TOMORROWS
vs
YESTERDAYS

Also by Andrew Keen

How to Fix the Future
The Internet Is Not the Answer
Digital Vertigo
The Cult of the Amateur

TOMORROWS
vs
YESTERDAYS

CONVERSATIONS IN DEFENSE
OF THE FUTURE

EDITED BY ANDREW KEEN

Atlantic Books
London

First published in Great Britain in 2019 by Atlantic Books,
an imprint of Atlantic Books Ltd.

1 2 3 4 5 6 7 8 9

A CIP catalogue record for this book is available from the British Library.

Hardback ISBN: 978 1 83895 112 2
E-book ISBN: 978 1 83895 113 9

Printed in Great Britain

Atlantic Books
An imprint of Atlantic Books Ltd
Ormond House
26–27 Boswell Street
London
WC1N 3JZ

www.atlantic-books.co.uk

FOR THE TOMORROWS OF TODAY

Contents

Part 3 DEMOCRACY AND ITS DIGITAL DISCONTENT

Part 4 FIXING THE FUTURE

Foreword

Digitalization is rapidly transforming our world. It is one of the major driving forces of change in the last two decades. It is so drastic and unsettling that it fosters fear, sarcasm, and pessimism, and a longing for the 'good old days' that felt more stable, less complex, and more humane. Of course, globalization, with its geopolitical conflicts, climate change, migration, and the shifting balance of economic power between West and East, is just as powerful a driver of change, but the boundless disruptive power of the digital revolution is behind it all.

When the internet was first made commonly available with the World Wide Web, we were all euphoric about its promise and the technologies that were developing alongside it. Everything was going to be easier and would allow us to reach higher, go faster, and further. On a societal level, the potential of a connected world, the proverbial global village, with shared knowledge and readily available information, was an exciting opportunity. The internet was thought to be the ultimate tool to ensure that democracy was finally going to spread across the globe like wildfire.

It was at this time that DLD was formed, to explore this new technology. In 2005, the year of the first DLD conference in Munich, there was no Twitter, no LinkedIn, and no Instagram. Facebook had just launched and Google was still a start-up, but every new digital company was praised as a game-changing business idea. We, as consumers, are still harvesting the positive outcomes of this wave of digitalization, which are being constantly reiterated in the shape of new products: real-time communication, from emailing and texting to video calls, custom search, online learning, video streaming, and online shopping and banking.

DLD connected the early digital adopters with the so-called 'old economy'. Some industries had a hard time adapting and many went under, while others were able to reinvent themselves or diversify their business model; DLD's parent company, Hubert Burda Media, was able to transform from a printing and publishing house into a digital media and technology company.

The rapid rise of social media in the first decade of the twenty-first century was embraced with enthusiasm. Mark Zuckerberg presented his social network at a DLD conference in Munich in 2009 in a conversation with David Kirkpatrick, who is featured in this book and has since become one of Facebook's most fervent critics.

When social media peaked, we were all posting, sharing, liking and commenting – which led to an entirely new way of communicating and sharing content. Once again, digital services were celebrated as new tools to further democratize the planet. The Arab Spring made Twitter the medium of the oppressed, as people were able to make themselves heard with poignant messages and live footage that escaped state-controlled media propaganda.

All the while, the companies running these 'democratization tools' gained unfathomable amounts of data about their users: their age, gender, and location, but also their likes, dislikes, habits, opinions, and beliefs – a treasure trove that they could convert directly into advertising revenue. Never before had it been possible to play messages to more or less the exact group of people who were supposed to hear them.

Most of us do not object to receiving special offers for products that we like, information about books that we might be interested in, or music that might match our taste. We do not object to being presented with news stories that are relevant to us on social media or to commentaries by people whose views we share. We do not object to our cell phone guiding us through cities. Most of us are willing to share our data if we get a useful and apparently free service in return.

But where do we draw the line? When does sharing our data with a company with whom we never signed a contract of service become an invasion of our privacy? When does reading news that reconfirms our beliefs and watching content that matches our taste become manipulation that traps us in a bubble and reduces our view of the world to a one-dimensional picture? And who is responsible for filtering what we see, read, and consume on digital platforms?

These are some of the questions that have in recent years dampened the euphoria about the digital age. Cambridge Analytica, Brexit, and the Christchurch mosque shootings have brought criticism of the digital age and its major players, and there is a massive reluctance to comply with the speed of change. Statements like 'Privacy is over', 'Tech giants are taking over every market and stifle innovation', 'Millions of people will lose their jobs due to smart machines', and 'Elections are won with so-called alternative facts' illustrate this development. This is much more than the eternal game of up and down, of yin and yang; with the digital age, we have opened Pandora's box. Alongside the excitement of digitalization, we have neglected to set the rules.

If history can teach us anything, it is that big societal and technological changes never come with a rule book attached – be it the invention of the printing press, industrialization, or the French Revolution. Rules are formed by trial and error; they are discussed and fought over. And every big change in history has seen winners and losers; the question is whether the digital age can be one that brings opportunities for everyone. One thing is for sure: we will not find the answers to the questions that the digital revolution raises by looking to the past. The procedures of the pre-digital world no longer work when it comes to ensuring competition, fairness, and prosperity.

We are at the point in the digital revolution where we have to step up and rewrite the rules. If the internet and social media are tools for democratization, then we should use them as such. If new technologies, from artificial intelligence to blockchain and quantum computing, have the potential to make the world better, then let us embrace and learn about them. Let us not be sheep going along with the crowd, not asking, knowing, or daring.

We believe that digital technologies play an integral part in solving, or at least mitigating, current issues – locally as well as globally. Digital communication platforms can help secure freedom of speech and encourage citizen engagement rather than spreading hate and disinformation, but we have to set the rules.

In the face of accelerating automation, online education can provide urgently needed specialist training to people who are untrained or don't have access to schools, but we have to provide stable internet access for everyone.

Digital technology can enhance public services, healthcare, farming, medicine, or mobility. It has the potential to save money and time and to make the world better, but we have to ensure it is secure, available to everyone, well regulated, and easy to use.

Machine learning, robotics, blockchain, and quantum computing all have huge innovation and business potential, but we have to ensure that we have the knowledge, the legal framework, and the investment power to make the most of it.

There is reason for optimism, and this goes to the core of what DLD is about. The digital age offers us boundless opportunities, but we need courage to seize them and to deal with the challenges along the way. Courage is the fuel that drives us to overcome boundaries – in our life, in business, and in our own mind. It gets us fired up to see the glass as half full rather than half empty, and to push for tomorrow rather than clinging to yesterday.

Steffi Czerny, Managing Director, DLD Media

TOMORROWS
vs
YESTERDAYS

INTRODUCTION

Tomorrow, and tomorrow, and tomorrow,
Creeps in this petty pace from day to day,
To the last syllable of recorded time;
And all our yesterdays have lighted fools
The way to dusty death.

Macbeth, Act V, Scene 5

A single conversation can sometimes trigger a series of further conversations each of which, in turn, can inspire many more. The original conversation that inspired this book was with Paul-Bernhard Kallen, the CEO of Burda Media, the German media conglomerate that runs the DLD series of conferences. I interviewed Paul for my last book, *How to Fix the Future*, and it was this conversation that flowered into the ones in this collection.

Over the last few years, whenever Paul and I have met – whether in Munich, New York City, Brussels, Palo Alto, or the other venues on the global DLD conference circuit – we've talked about the most pressing questions and challenges of our age. Our conversations have been about the threat and promise of Silicon Valley, the current crisis of liberal democracy, the growing economic inequality between rich and poor, our narcissistic social media culture, and the threat of AI. Whatever our specific subject, however, the overarching theme of our conversations has always been the same: how can we learn from the analog twentieth century to shape a better digital twenty-first century? Technology, and particularly the opportunities and challenges of digital technology, has always been at the heart of our conversations. The digital revolution, we both believe, is what's shaping the core problems and opportunities of our age.

While Paul and I share a concern about the current direction of the digital revolution, neither of us have fallen into the trap of idealizing an imaginary analog past. We aren't, I hope, just another couple of middle-aged white guys who want to return to the imaginary idyll of our childhoods. So our conversations, which share the optimistic, forward-thinking spirit of Steffi Czerny's DLD conferences, have never been nostalgic for a supposedly halcyon analog twentieth-century world that can't, at the flick of a switch, be reinvented in the digital twenty-first century. We agree that we can learn from the past, but realize that you can't turn back the clock; if history teaches us anything, we know, it's that we should focus on tomorrow rather than yesterday.

I could have written a book in the style of Louis Malle's 1981 movie *My Dinner with Andre* and called it *My Conversations with Paul*, but rather than transcribing our own conversations, Paul wanted to democratize the project. He suggested that I start a podcast in which I discussed the great questions and challenges of our age with leading technologists, writers, entrepreneurs, and investors around the world. And so, with the help of Paul's business development lieutenant, Sophie Ahrens, and Steffi Czerny, Alexandra Schiel, and Heiko Schlott at DLD, I started a podcast series entitled 'Keen on Democracy' that has built upon the themes of my original conversations with Paul, and particularly on the idea that the way to fix the future isn't to retreat into a romanticized past.

In the traditional narrative, the twenty-first-century podcast comes after the twentieth-century book, but the story of this book is the reverse. Having launched a weekly podcast series that has been downloaded by many thousands of listeners, we decided to transform it into a physical book; the conversations that you are about to read were all originally broadcast as part of the 'Keen on Democracy' podcast.

Unlike digital media, books are not infinite storage systems. Only so many pages can exist between a book's covers, so not all the podcasts from the series could be included in this book.

After a spirited debate, we selected the 18 interviews which we believed best captured the questions and challenges of our digital age. If you enjoy the conversations in this book, I urge you to listen to all the interviews in the podcast series by subscribing online.

One of the conversations from the podcast series that didn't make it into this collection was with David Goodhart, the British author of the controversial 2017 book *Road to Somewhere*. Goodhart told me that in our globalized world, where twentieth-century political distinctions like 'left' and 'right' and 'liberal' and 'conservative' appear archaic, the key difference is between what he calls 'somewheres' and 'anywheres'. And there's no doubt that, in today's age of Trump, Putin, and Brexit, his distinction between a global cosmopolitan elite (the 'anywheres') and more fixed communities (the 'somewheres') helps to make sense of the shouting matches that define our times.

However, I think there's an even better way to frame the divisions of today's world. Rather than Goodhart's 'somewheres' versus 'anywheres' split, the most important division of our age is, I believe, between what I dub the 'tomorrows' and the 'yesterdays'. This division is encapsulated by how an individual answers a simple question: can we trust the future?

The 'tomorrows' – people such as Paul-Bernhard Kallen, Steffi Czerny, and the thinkers featured in this book – believe that the future, for all its problems, can and indeed must be better than the past. The 'tomorrows' trust the twenty-first century; the 'yesterdays', by contrast, have no trust in the future; rather, they are nostalgic for something they believe we've lost and want to return to this imaginary past.

This idea of yesterdays and tomorrows was triggered by my podcast conversation with Richard Stengel, the former editor of *Time* magazine. Stengel tells a memorable story about an encounter with Vladimir Putin:

'When I was editor of *Time*, we made Vladimir Putin Person of the Year in 2007 and he agreed to an interview. We went to Moscow, and from there we drove out to his dacha outside Moscow for lunch, but he kept us waiting for six hours so it turned into dinner.

'After the interview we had this great British photographer named Platon take his picture. Platon is this kind of elfin fellow and while he's taking the picture, his schtick is that he talks about The Beatles and just before he takes the picture, he asks the person what their favorite Beatles song is?

'Putin had not said a word of English during the whole interview and when Platon turned to him and asked, "What's your favorite Beatles song?" Putin, without missing a beat, said, "Yesterday".'

With his nostalgia for the twentieth-century Soviet Union, Vladimir Putin epitomizes the twenty-first-century 'yesterday man'. He is, as Peter Pomerantsev reminds us, the pioneer of a nostalgic ideology that doesn't trust the future – no wonder his favorite Beatles song is 'Yesterday'.

In contrast with Vladimir Putin, the people featured in this book are united in wanting to trust the future, but that doesn't mean that they agree on how to fix or shape it. For example, some of my interviewees trust the regulators to solve the most pressing issues of our digital age, while others believe that this can be better achieved through individuals or corporations. Some trust the United States as the pioneer of a better future, while others have more faith in the European model. Some want to split up the Silicon Valley leviathans, but others don't. Some want more direct democracy, while others favor representative democracy. Some want more market capitalism, and some want less.

We've divided the interviews into four sections:

- We begin with conversations featuring Shoshana Zuboff, Maria Ressa, John Borthwick, and Rana Foroohar that identify the core problems and challenges of our digital age.
- The second section explores the ideas of David Kirkpatrick, Douglas Rushkoff, Peter Sunde, Eli Pariser, and Kenn Cukier, focusing on the failure of the internet revolution to realize its ambitious goals.

- The third part presents interviews with Peter Pomerantsev, Catherine Fieschi, Ian Bremmer, Martin Wolf, and Ece Temelkuran that explore the current crisis of democracy and untangle the complex relationship between populism and digital media.
- The final section includes conversations with Carl Benedikt Frey, Toomas Ilves, Richard Stengel, and Scott Galloway that focus on possible solutions to the challenges of our digital age.

I suggested earlier in this introduction that conversations can be viral. My single conversation with Paul-Bernhard Kallen triggered a series of podcasts which resulted in the eighteen conversations in this book, but that should be the beginning rather than the end of the conversation. This book, in the spirit of the DLD conferences, is part of an ongoing conversation about the future. Your job is to read these interviews and then start your own conversation – that's the shortcut to a better tomorrow.

PART 1

THE CRISIS

SHOSHANA ZUBOFF

In 2018, before her brilliant book *The Age of Surveillance Capitalism: The Fight for a Human Future at the New Frontier of Power* was published, Shoshana Zuboff sent me a review copy. Astonished by its fluency, elegance, and passion, I wrote a glowing pre-publication quote comparing the book to *The Origins of Totalitarianism* by Hannah Arendt. Many other reviewers were equally impressed by her erudition and intelligence, with some even suggesting that it was the most important book yet published in the twenty-first century.

I admit that I was a little nervous when Shoshana agreed to be interviewed by me at my home in Berkeley, California, for the 'Keen on Democracy' podcast. I hadn't met her before and was keen to talk to the woman behind this immense book; I was pleased to discover that Shoshana is as fluent, elegant, and passionate in person as is *The Age of Surveillance Capitalism*. She is a remarkable woman and thinker, and I hope this interview does justice to her brilliance.

Andrew Keen: The most acclaimed new book about technology in 2019 is *The Age of Surveillance Capitalism: The Fight for a Human Future at the New Frontier of Power* by Shoshana Zuboff. The *Irish Times* called it 'The most important book of the twenty-first century'; a number of other authors have compared it to *Capital in the Twenty-First Century* by Thomas Piketty in terms of its critique of the digital revolution. Shoshana Zuboff, congratulations; have you been surprised with this huge acclaim for your book?

Shoshana Zuboff: The book has been a long project of intense study and concentration for many years, and seven years of writing. I think as an author, one always hopes but one never knows. A lot of things worked out in terms of the timing for this book, because I think we're finally at a moment when many of us in the United States, Europe, and around the world are already beginning to have doubts about this whole digital milieu – who is running it, who is controlling it, how is it affecting our lives, is it just, is it unjust? A lot of people are trying to get their minds around this and are trying to understand it and put words to a general sense of malaise – something is not right, but we don't know what to call it.

Andrew Keen: So you've called it 'surveillance capitalism'. What does that mean?

Shoshana Zuboff: Surveillance capitalism refers to the social relations that are required in order for this kind of economic logic to be successful, so I call it 'the social relations of the one-way mirror'. In other words, if the methods and mechanisms of surveillance capitalists were out in the open, if they were known to us, we would be rebelling. We would be resisting. We would be saying no, and they would not be making any money.

Andrew Keen: So who are the surveillance capitalists? Is it Google? Is it Facebook? Is it Amazon? Is it Apple?

Shoshana Zuboff: Surveillance capitalism was discovered, invented, and elaborated at Google in 2000, 2001, during the dot-com bust. From there it migrated to Facebook with Sheryl Sandberg, and from there it became the default option in Silicon Valley and in the tech sector in general, but what's most interesting is that it is no longer a function of a single corporation or a few big tech corporations or even of the tech sector. This is now an economic logic that has spread across the normal and has become the gold standard that people are chasing in virtually every economic sector: insurance, retail, health, finance, all the way to automobile manufacturing, where the great industrialists of the twentieth century got their start – because of course, Ford Motor was the crucible of twentieth-century mass production. And now it's the CEO of

Ford Motor who is publicly discussing that company's move toward what I describe as surveillance capitalism.

Andrew Keen: I always imagined surveillance capitalism as being built around the business model of free, but are you suggesting that it can also involve people selling products and then building data and the disruption of privacy on the back of that?

Shoshana Zuboff: We blew by free a long time ago. First of all, we pay for the devices that participate in surveillance capitalism and represent the interface for these vast supply chains of behavioral data that are shunted to machine intelligence operations. We pay for the phone. We pay for the television set that listens to our conversation. We pay for the mattress that has the sensors in it that siphons data to the Nest thermostat that siphons data to the Nest security system that just a couple of weeks ago was revealed to have a microphone built into it.

Andrew Keen: And Nest, of course, is owned by Google.

Shoshana Zuboff: So that's one way that we're paying for it, but the insurance industry now is what they call 'behavioral underwriting', where they are trying to tap into data streams about our real-time behavior, as well as other sources of personal information, and use that for their evaluation of their premiums.

Andrew Keen: So in the old days, in the industrial age, everyone bought the same insurance and the insurance company didn't know too much about you. These days, in the age of surveillance capitalism, they'll know how many times we go to the gym, whether we smoke, what we eat, where we walk, if we walk at all. Is that what surveillance capitalism is?

Shoshana Zuboff: It's the complete destruction of privacy, and I would stress that in order to have privacy, we have to have the right to make decisions about the boundaries of our own experience. And what surveillance capitalism does carefully and intentionally is engineer their methods and systems to bypass our awareness so we never know what, when, or how they are claiming our personal experience as raw material to translate into personal data, to ship to their machines, to create predictions about our future behavior.

And because we are intentionally engineered to be ignorant of this whole structure, we have lost the right to put boundaries on our own experience. We've lost the right to decide what is private and what is public. We've lost the right to exercise our own sense of self-determination and our own individual autonomy. This is intolerable because when we just zoom out a little bit, we understand that one can't even think of the possibility of a democratic society without the assumption that we have citizens who have the ability to make autonomous moral judgments. And in a whole variety of ways, compelled by their own economic imperatives, surveillance capitalism is on a collision course with human freedom.

Andrew Keen: Join the dots between the shift toward authoritarianism – Brexit, Trump, Putin, China – and surveillance capitalism.

Shoshana Zuboff: Well, those are a lot of dots.

Andrew Keen: But is there a single path between those dots, or is it an interconnected series of dots?

Shoshana Zuboff: All of those dots, certainly China, Cambridge Analytica, and what we now understand to be the Russian intelligence interventions in these elections, derive from one central source, and that is the two decades of careful invention and elaboration of the methods and mechanisms of surveillance capitalism.

What Cambridge Analytica, China, and Russia represent is a way of commandeering these mechanisms and methods and pivoting them a couple of degrees toward commercial outcomes instead of political outcomes. But they all derive from the same source, and when you understand what Cambridge Analytica was up to, those methods that they used had begun to be developed by academic researchers as early as 2010, 2011, and were already being adapted by surveillance capitalists. And even after the Cambridge Analytica revelations in March 2018, we have a leaked document from Facebook in April 2018 that is a beautiful description of Facebook doing what Cambridge Analytica did, and doing it on steroids.

Beginning with Cambridge Analytica, what we see there is a day in the life, routine life, of a solid, self-respecting surveillance capitalist.

Andrew Keen: So what do we do about it? The subtitle of your book is *The Fight for a Human Future*, and your definition of a human future is one with human agency. How do we re-establish human agency in a world where it seems as if we've lost it? Where do we begin?

Shoshana Zuboff: We begin with democracy.

Andrew Keen: And democracy is the purest manifestation of human agency, the will of the people?

Shoshana Zuboff: Everything depends upon democracy. We're living in a moment, in the United States and Europe and other parts of the world, where democracy appears to be under siege, in a way that many of us thought was unimaginable. Democratic institutions are being tested and some have fallen, even within Western Europe which we thought was inviolable to these kinds of threats.

Andrew Keen: Well, how is it going to work? How are we going to get democracy back? Are we grabbing it back? The human future is something we have to seize – it's not going to be given to us.

Shoshana Zuboff: I talk to young people a lot and what I've come to understand is that a lot of young people have the idea that democracy is like a rock, it's like a mountain. It's there when you're born and it stays there and it's immovable. But that's not what democracy is. My metaphor for it is more like the hoop game that kids played in the late nineteenth, early twentieth century, where you've got a hoop and you roll it and you run after it and you try to keep it from teetering and falling over. Every generation faces the work of running after that hoop and preventing it from teetering and falling over, and that's where we are now. And I believe that we've been in worse jams; look at the bloody story of the twentieth century. My grandparents and my great-grandparents have been in worse jams, and we found our way out of them.

Andrew Keen: Is this another war, Shoshana? Is this equivalent to war in some way, this fight against surveillance capitalism?

Shoshana Zuboff: Well, Chris Wylie, the Cambridge Analytica whistleblower, to whom we owe a great debt, called it 'information warfare'. And the thing about this information warfare is that it's not states facing off against one another, soldier to soldier, military to military. When we talk about surveillance capitalism, it's actually private surveillance capital facing off against all of us.

Andrew Keen: So is it an equivalent, if we want to think of things in historical terms, of the nineteenth century and the fight against what Marx called bourgeois capitalism or industrial capitalism?

Shoshana Zuboff: Let me give you an analogy. Earlier in the nineteenth century in Britain you had the term 'aristocracy' and you had the term 'wealthy class' and then for everyone else you had one term: the 'lower classes'. And in the lower classes you had bankers and merchants and shopkeepers and laborers and paupers and everything in between. And it took decades for the idea of the laborer to emerge as an identity. They identified with one another as a collective identity because they understood their shared economic interests.

Andrew Keen: And is that what we need to do today? We have to think of ourselves as data laborers?

Shoshana Zuboff: No, let me amend that. Today we are called 'users'.

Andrew Keen: Or consumers?

Shoshana Zuboff: Yes, and we didn't start off by calling ourselves users. They call us users.

Andrew Keen: It's interesting that people also describe drug addicts as users.

Shoshana Zuboff: Exactly, and I don't think that's an accident. So we thought that we were using these services that are free; we thought we were using social media. We thought we were using search; in fact, they are using us. So here we are, the great unwashed users, just like the lower classes.

Andrew Keen: What's a better word? How should we be rethinking ourselves?

Shoshana Zuboff: Where we are now is understanding not just our economic interests, as was the case a century ago, when we understood our interests as laborers, as employees, and also as consumers. And we came together in those identities to address the challenges of twentieth-century industrial capitalism. And that was the institutions of collective bargaining, of trade unions, the right to strike. We used our identities to pressure our elected officials and draw on the resources of our democratic institutions for new legislation and new regulatory regimes. We outlawed child labor. We outlawed unsafe working conditions. We created legislation that governed the working week and wages, and we righted the incredible asymmetry of power that existed at that time. We made it something tolerable that approached an equilibrium that we could call market democracy.

Now we are way out of that equilibrium again. We've entered the twenty-first century already disfigured institutionally. We talked about the threat to democracy from below, which is the threat to human autonomy and free will because of the way in which surveillance capitalists intervene in our behavior to help manage us toward its guaranteed outcomes, which is one of its critical imperatives. But I also want to point out that we have the threats from above because in the first two decades of the twenty-first century these institutions of private capital have created asymmetries of knowledge that are beyond anything we've ever seen in human history.

So this is not only economic justice that is challenged here, as we saw a century ago; this is justice about who gets to know things, who decides who gets to know things, who decides who decides who gets to know things, and now that we live in an information civilization, if we aren't able to know things, we aren't able to earn a living or function effectively.

Andrew Keen: So what you're saying is that the old tools of taming capitalism, of anti-trust, of breaking up large companies, and of more regulation are probably not sufficient in the age of surveillance capitalism? It requires new strategies and new ways of thinking, organizing, and conceiving of ourselves?

Shoshana Zuboff: We have not adequately implemented the anti-trust laws that exist, and those laws are important because surveillance capitalists can also be ruthless capitalists. And there are monopoly issues and there are anti-competitive issues and we should implement those laws. We have not implemented our privacy laws – in 2011 the Federal Trade Commission made a consent decree with Facebook that has not been enforced. So all these laws should be enforced and they are necessary, but once we understand the specific economic logic of surveillance capitalism – its mechanisms, the way it works, and the fact that it unilaterally takes private human experience for translation into behavioral data – no matter how much we implement anti-trust, we're not going to stop those mechanisms.

So we also need to build on what has gone before and to invent the kinds of laws and regulatory regimes that are going to interrupt and even outlaw the mechanisms of surveillance capitalism. For example, people talk about data ownership. Well, once we get comfortable with the idea that we're producing labor and we should own and be paid for it, we have omitted a very important first step: by saying we should own the data, we've essentially legitimated the fact that those data should exist in the first place, when those data exist illegitimately.

When you're walking down the street, there are cameras that are doing facial recognition, and those cameras are funneled into these private supply chains for surveillance capitalism.

Andrew Keen: I don't like to use *inevitable* but given the nature of Moore's Law and given the devices that we all use, isn't the personal data you're talking about inevitable? Isn't the question how does it get used? You can't get rid of data, can you?

Shoshana Zuboff: No one wants to get rid of data – the whole point of the digital was that we would have a tremendous amount of data that would help us to improve our lives. But we're talking about millions and millions of data points, personal information that is processed by Facebook, Google, and others on a daily basis, not to fix healthcare, to address the climate crisis, or to invent something that will fundamentally make hunger impossible, but to improve its ability to predict our behavior and to sell those predictions into its new behavioral futures markets to business customers who want to lay bets on what we're going to do now, soon, and later.

Andrew Keen: Should that just be illegal then?

Shoshana Zuboff: Yes it should. Here we have this hugely lucrative form of capitalism that does not require us as customers, that has massive knowledge about us, that is not used for us, that knows everything about us while we know almost nothing about it, all of this for the benefit of business customers and not for us.

This is a perversion of what our hopes for the digital were. If you go back to that window between 1996 and 2003, before the world caught onto surveillance capitalism, before Google IPOed in 2004, what you see are tremendous projects for the smart home, projects for telemedicine, and all of the assumptions were that we were going to get all this tremendous data going to the occupant of the home or to the patient and the patient's physician. Those are the people who get the data, figure out what it means, and if and how it's shared. That was the promise of the digital: empowerment, democratization, emancipatory, radical improvement of our lives, and that is the promise that we have lost.

This has nothing to do with the digital technology itself. The data to improve our lives does not depend upon invading our boundaries and measuring the muscles in our faces in order to compute our emotional state in order to have predictions of our behavior, in order to sell it to businesses who can then make money knowing what we are likely to do or want or say.

Andrew Keen: Shoshana, have we reached the political tipping point here? Your book has been enormously successful and Elizabeth Warren quite recently came out very explicitly about breaking up the large tech-monopolies. Is this now a mainstream political issue? Is it indeed the political issue of the future?

Shoshana Zuboff: I think we are living in a moment when it has become a mainstream political issue, and the challenge for us is to keep it that way. I've gone through the analysis, and when you look at very specific things that surveillance capitalists do and at very specific things that happen under the Chinese state as it takes the capabilities of this data and the subsequent ability to modify human behavior at scale, the differences are not very large but are nuanced rather than dramatic.

Andrew Keen: So you're applauding what Warren is saying?

Shoshana Zuboff: I'm applauding the fact that we have a woman who is a candidate for the democratic presidential nomination who is making this an issue, and she's not alone – there are others who are doing the same. And they're doing so because we have come to understand that this is a threat, not only to us as individuals, but to the possibility of the endurance of our democracy.

Andrew Keen: So we end as we began, with the centrality of democracy?

Shoshana Zuboff: Let's remind everybody that democracy is the one form of government created in human history that says people should govern themselves. It is not perfect. It goes through its ups and downs and we fight for it and keep it robust. But for literally millennia people have died and sacrificed for this idea; it is imperfect and it has never been perfectly realized. But this is an ideal that as a species we cannot afford to give up.

JOHN BORTHWICK

I feel like I've been talking to my friend John Borthwick forever. Whenever I'm in New York City, I go to the Meatpacking District on Manhattan's Lower East Side to talk to the Betaworks CEO about the state of the world. We don't agree about everything, although over the last few years our views about the digital economy have become increasingly similar.

Given John's enthusiasm for conversation, it's not surprising that he's opened a new kind of talking shop in Betaworks Studios, a social and networking club for what he calls the 'builders' of our new economy. This interview took place there, and I hope it captures the mutual respect between John and me that makes my conversations with him both valuable and fun.

Andrew Keen: John Borthwick, co-founder and CEO of Betaworks, is democracy in crisis?

John Borthwick: I think democracy is in retreat right now, and I do think it's in crisis. I think we went through this period after the Berlin Wall came down for 20 to 25 years where democracy was on the march and now, for a whole series of reasons including technology, I think it is proving to be not the only and maybe not the best means to govern a country.

Andrew Keen: What are the most worrying examples of the contemporary crisis today?

John Borthwick: I think China by far. The massive change that we've seen in China in the last 20 to 25 years – the growth of the middle class, the complete rise of China we thought would inevitably lead to a democratic China and it didn't. I remember about five years ago I thought what was going to do it was urbanization and the environmental problems in China – you had smog over the cities and tension between rural and urban, and you now look at Xi Jinping and he is somebody who has gained more power than anybody has in probably 100 years in China, so I think China is a pre-eminent example.

Andrew Keen: Is China proof of Samuel Huntington's un-popular argument of the time, that might now be a bit more acceptable, of this clash of civilizations – the idea that the

Chinese just aren't going to be democratic and the West for cultural and historical reasons are democratic?

John Borthwick: I think that placing it in the context of political philosophy may be premature, but I think China is setting an example that you could see spreading. To take another very important country, India, which has inherited democracy from the West, I would imagine that today there will be a fair amount of people in India who will be saying that maybe this is not the best way to govern.

Andrew Keen: Because the Chinese are succeeding and the West is embarrassing itself?

John Borthwick: Right, and the Chinese have managed to pull their people into a rising economy far faster than the Indians have.

Andrew Keen: What is the role of technology, and particularly digital technology, in China's very sharp shift away from democracy?

John Borthwick: We started off with no connectivity and then we went to the Great Wall of China, which censored connectivity and now what we have is one of the most connected societies in the world. And when you talk about the rise of urban China and think about what's happened in the cities, and about last mile logistics and how technology has enabled that, you have a marketplace that is in many cases far more advanced than what we have here in the West, for a whole series of reasons. One is they went straight to mobile – there was no desktop era there, so they skipped that. So you have a more advanced mobile experience there, but then coupled with that I think when you look at machine learning, AI, and data collection you can see that China is positioning itself from a research, capital, engineering, and a company creation standpoint to be a leader in the world – and they have a good shot at it.

Andrew Keen: Everyone talked about this jump to mobile as being empowering for the people, but what you're suggesting is that China's jump to mobile has empowered not the people but the state, with all this surveillance technology?

John Borthwick: Yes, and I think we can see that surveillance technology here in the West, too, but here it's being controlled by corporations.

Andrew Keen: Like who?

John Borthwick: Like Facebook, Amazon, Google.

Andrew Keen: At the DLD New York event in May, you explicitly compared politics and what's going on in China with Facebook. Do you still stick to that?

John Borthwick: Yes, I do. I think Zuckerberg and Facebook as a company today has more control over a larger segment of the world's population than people understand and appreciate, and more control than most heads of states have over their countries.

Andrew Keen: But Facebook isn't in the business of controlling what people say? Zuckerberg doesn't care whether or not people love Facebook – he just wants them to use Facebook.

John Borthwick: Yeah, but I think that when you control the means of distribution of what people are saying, and I'm talking about countries like Sri Lanka or Myanmar or Nigeria, countries that ten to fifteen years ago had almost no internet connectivity and now have 20 or 30 per cent of the population connected to the internet, and almost 100 per cent of that is through Facebook. And so if you control the distribution point and then if you think about how the news feed is structured and the kind of content that the news feed is optimized for, it is a control of voice. And it's a control of a population in a very different way than an Orwell or a Xi would have necessarily thought about, but it's a technocratic control of a population.

Andrew Keen: What do you think of Amazon pioneering various kinds of new surveillance technologies?

John Borthwick: On one hand, I have tremendous respect for these companies and their ability to innovate at that scale. The companies we just talked about, Facebook and Amazon, are innovating in ways that large companies do not typically innovate.

Andrew Keen: So you would make the explicit comparison between Facebook and China, but you wouldn't do it between Amazon and China or Google and China?

John Borthwick: I think you can draw the parallel with Facebook because of its impact on the way that people are actually talking to one another, because it intersects with the conversational flow of how I connect with my tribe, which is inevitably going to be my Facebook-influenced or -controlled tribe. I think most of what Amazon is doing is in the purchase sphere and most of what Google is doing is in the search and discovery sphere, and I think their impact is less for that reason.

Andrew Keen: What do you make of Eric Schmidt's prediction that in five or ten years we're in danger of having two internets, one controlled by China and one by the West?

John Borthwick: Well, I think that we already have a public internet that is under a lot of pressure and shrinking in size, from an attention standpoint.

Andrew Keen: So you don't buy the Schmidt bifurcation of the internet? You think it's more complicated than that?

John Borthwick: Well, I think it's already happened. So I don't buy that it *will* happen. I think it's happened now.

Andrew Keen: So we're already there; we're already in this 'splinternet'?

John Borthwick: Yeah – there's a Russian internet, there's a Chinese internet. And I think there's a Facebook internet.

Andrew Keen: How does Russia and Putin fit into the narrative of the crisis of democracy? Are they important players or are they just troublemakers, mosquitoes on the body of democracy?

John Borthwick: Well, I think the emerging economies and the transition that China, India, and Russia went through in the 1990s and the 2000s are instructive for many other countries who are moving toward modernization, because in the West we had the assumption that we could export 'democracy light' into these countries, and I think Russia was the first example of that.

I remember when the Berlin Wall came down and before that, growing up with this sense of Europe being divided. The first time I went to East Germany it was post the Berlin Wall coming down and it was remarkable. The world had suddenly opened up.

Andrew Keen: And that has shut down now, the world is no longer open?

John Borthwick: Yes, I think that closed down. I think that Putin has very effectively…

Andrew Keen: Sabotaged democracy?

John Borthwick: You go back to the clash of civilizations and I think the assumption that we've made, that it is the natural end state, is something that people are questioning. It may be at some point, but I think that if you sit down with Putin or with Xi, I think they would question that and say, 'This is a better system and it's working better for us right now.'

Andrew Keen: Do you think the Russian and Chinese people would agree, the typical Russian or Chinese citizen?

John Borthwick: I don't know – I don't want to speak for them. I have an American friend who has lived in China for the last 15 years, and he thinks it's pretty great.

Andrew Keen: Well, you're an Anglo-Frenchman who has lived in America for what, 30 years – what do you make of what's happening here? Should we be worried about American democracy? Is Trump just a reality television star who seized the stage for four years, or are there bigger structural issues here?

John Borthwick: Look, I think that in the broader swathe of history, I believe that the checks and balances that have been built into the system here in the United States will endure. I do think that politics has been changed by Trump and by what we're going through now, but I'm not sitting here worried about the future of American democracy. I think that will endure.

As for what happens to the Republican Party, I think that part of it will snap back. I've always been fascinated in this country about the inability of third parties to start up and I wonder if this could be a time when third parties could emerge. It's hard to see this but I think that Trump is a symptom, not the cause, and I think the underlying cause has to do with how technology is transforming society.

Andrew Keen: So what can technology do to strengthen democracy? It seems to have played a role in undermining it or weakening it in some ways. What can we do in technology to support the future of democracy?

John Borthwick: I think technology is both the answer and the problem. Generally, I think the way we're building things needs to change. Very specifically the agile, fast, 'break things and figure it out later'…

Andrew Keen: The Zuckerberg model?

John Borthwick: Yes, I think Zuckerberg has done an amazing job of that, but I would say more generally that it's agile development. It's why I called this place Betaworks – because we believe betas work. So that rapid 'fuck it, ship it, just test it' methodology needs to change and adapt. One of the parallels I think about is the methodology of agile development, which is basically akin to the scientific method of stating a hypothesis and then having a rapid process to test that hypothesis and see if it works. And if you get product market fit, you go from there.

And I think if you look at medicine and science, we have over the span of a few centuries in Western medicine worked out how to have a test and trial methodology to figure out if something is wrong with you and then try and fix it, but around that we also have some sense of guard rails of values. How are we going to actually think about what we will do and what we won't do? We've got to start thinking about what we won't do, so when we think about AI or biohacking or brain-machine interfaces, what are the parameters or things which you will not do?

Andrew Keen: More regulation?

John Borthwick: I don't think it's necessarily regulation.

Andrew Keen: Self-regulation or government?

John Borthwick: Government regulation will play a role here because I think there are some things, when you talk about Crispr and 'biology as data' and when you think about changing the very nature of our species, there will be some regulatory boundaries that we want to define and push up against, but I think a lot of this is about us seeing if we can, as an industry of people who are building things, change the process by which we build, to insert a sense of intentionality, and to understand how we can place the human at the center of what we're trying to build.

Andrew Keen: So we should be a bit more moral in tech?

John Borthwick: I use the analogy of the bicycles of the mind. Steve Jobs was talking about how he was looking through some *Scientific American* magazines and there was an analysis of mammals and speed. And the human being was way behind a whole bunch of mammals in terms of our ability to move, to run.

But then you put up a human being on a bicycle and everything changes, and so Jobs was talking about the fact that computers are bicycles for the mind. And what I love about that is that it places the human being at the center and says that the machine's job is to expand on the human. Us thinking about technology as expanding on the human, and thinking about how we can have more thought that the implications of the technology we're building, is part of what we need to change as builders.

Andrew Keen: A few years ago in tech we used to say that politicians needed to learn to be more agile. Are you suggesting now that agility is a problem and that the tech community can learn from traditional politics and politicians? That there could be more of a symbiosis between politics and tech?

John Borthwick: The software is in societies so we need to think carefully about what society we're going to create out of that. We as engineers also need to learn how to talk to other constituents, whether they be politicians, whether they be designers, whether they be doctors, whether they be teachers; instead of just replumbing the process of education, we have to start figuring out how you can start working with teachers to enable them to teach better.

And the same with politicians – we've deindustrialized so much of the creation process, but we need to get deeper into that process of development.

Andrew Keen: What's one thing that we could do right now to strengthen democracy; what would it be, in the short term? Not just long-term education reform – shut Facebook down?

John Borthwick: I turned off my Facebook a while ago, after the Cambridge Analytica thing. I went to Facebook and downloaded my data and I went through it all. I was barely using this service, but I was amazed about how much data they had gathered. When I shut down my Facebook account, the only thing I felt before I clicked the button was this sense of panic. And then I just deleted it and felt a sense of relief at just being free of one of those latent burdens that I don't need, because I don't have that buzzing in the corner of my notifications or anywhere and I don't need it.

Andrew Keen: So maybe everyone should delete something to focus more, to have more attention and to perhaps be more responsible citizens?

John Borthwick: Yeah. I was sitting down with a friend yesterday and they had a cigarette warning sticker on the back of their phone: 'This device can seriously harm your health'. And I think these devices have been incredibly enabling, but I also think they've narrowed and changed the way that we live and communicate, in ways that are far more profound than any of us could have imagined.

MARIA RESSA

I first met Maria Ressa when she invited me to speak at a conference in Manila in 2010, and we've been friends ever since. Neither of us knew that she would become one of the world's best-known opponents of twenty-first-century neo-authoritarianism, and I was particularly thrilled when she was made *Time* magazine's Person of the Year in 2018 for her defense of journalistic truth in our age of misinformation.

But Maria's fame has come at a price: she has been embroiled in a vicious legal conflict with the Duterte regime in the Philippines, and the threat of jail has hung over her for the last couple of years. Yet, in spite of all the vitriol and lies directed at her, she remains the same energetic and principled journalist that I first met in 2010. I hope this interview, conducted in Manila in September 2019, is a testament to her bravery and intelligence.

Andrew Keen: Maria Ressa, why do you think *Time* magazine made you their Person of the Year last year?

Maria Ressa: I was one of four journalists that they put on their cover, and they called us 'The Guardians of Truth'. And when I saw the four of us, there was Jamal Khashoggi who was brutally murdered and it had shocked the entire world, and the two journalists from Myanmar were at that point still in prison, and then you had *The Capital Gazette*, where journalists there were murdered. And that's when I realized that I was the only one who is free and alive, and I thought is this how tough it is to be a journalist today?

Andrew Keen: When did you recognize the real harm that social media was doing to democracy?

Maria Ressa: I think everything changed in 2015, which was when Facebook introduced Instant Articles, which brought newsgroups onto the platform, but there was no change in the algorithm. So you were using algorithms about jokes and what you had for dinner to determine what facts were, and that's when the gaming happened. At the end of 2015, Rappler and three other newsgroups in the Philippines went onto Instant Articles, and that's when I realized. By February 2016, which is when the campaign was ongoing, I took us off Instant Articles and began to study how social media was being used.

Duterte was elected in May 2016. A month later you had Brexit. In November you had Donald Trump, and then a short while later Jair Bolsonaro in Brazil.

Andrew Keen: So you were amongst the first journalists to expose the way in which these new authoritarians were gaming social media?

Maria Ressa: We lived it, and we had the data. In July 2016, one month after Duterte was elected, we saw the weaponization of social media. When the campaign accounts were used to pound perceived critics into silence, the first ones they attacked were anyone on social media, on Facebook, who questioned the drug war, which began in July 2016.

The second targets were institutions who were the truth-tellers: journalists, newsgroups. The third were opposition politicians. But what was interesting to me was that we watched this pivot, which was like a complete turnaround from social media for social good, to attacks that I didn't think were part of the Filipino psyche.

We were working with a research group in 2017 that coined the term 'patriotic trolling', online, state-sponsored hate that is meant to silence perceived critics. In our case, we began a campaign called #noplaceforhate in August. We were very naive because I thought at that point that people were just being angry; I didn't realize how systematic the whole thing was.

And when we began collecting the data, by the end of August I went to Facebook and said, 'This is really alarming – you've got to look at this.' And when we showed them that 26 fake accounts could actually influence three million others and what messaging was being used, I hoped they would take action. I told them that if they didn't do anything, Trump could win. We all laughed because in August 2016 it didn't look like Trump could win, and then in November they asked me for the data again.

Andrew Keen: And do you think this was initially pioneered in Russia or in China?

Maria Ressa: It follows Russian disinformation. By the end of September I had given the data to Facebook and was hoping they would either do something or give me the data back, but I never heard from them. I waited a month and a half, and then at the end of September I told them that we would go ahead with the story.

Andrew Keen: Was that a threat to them, in a sense?

Maria Ressa: I don't know if it was a threat – the people I spoke with were Policy and Sales. They weren't in charge of the data, and one of the things I've learned is that they don't have data people in our part of the world. But when we came out with the series – this was the first globally that looked at the propaganda war, the weaponization of the internet – Facebook was what was used.

Filipinos have spent most time on social media globally, four years running, and Facebook really is our internet, so when nothing happened we came out with the story. And that was October 2016; almost immediately the attacks began and they were increased exponentially. At the beginning I tried to respond to some of them and then I realized they weren't really interested in an answer. At some point the attacks happened so frequently, and this was through the night, that I started counting them. And I came to an average of 90 hate messages per hour. That's a new weapon against journalists.

Andrew Keen: And this hate was orchestrated by the regime?

Maria Ressa: We were able to show that it connected directly to two people who were pro-Duterte bloggers, but they were given government offices.

Andrew Keen: Do you think the fact that you're a woman and these neo-authoritarians are men is significant?

Maria Ressa: I think what's happened is that the populism they rode on pushed progress on the gender front back to the Stone Age. In the Philippines, the attacks of the president are sexist at best and misogynistic at worst. And it brought out the worst in our men and in our society. We've taken so many steps back and the attacks online are vicious. We now have a database that we call 'the shark tank'. It's about a terabyte large, and in that database women are attacked ten times more than men.

Andrew Keen: These regimes tend to be prehistoric in ideological terms – they're not very sophisticated. They tend to be nostalgic and reactionary, but they're highly sophisticated when it comes to tech. Why and how is that?

Maria Ressa: I think this is a form of digital colonialism. What enabled these types of mass manipulation were the social media platforms, the American giants that came in. It's the way they were designed, a kind of micro-targeting of advertising that offers an insidious way of manipulating that takes away free will in many instances.

The second wave are digital companies like Cambridge Analytica, which makes sense. If the giant tech platforms enable mass manipulation, who does the manipulation? And that brings power and money. Cambridge Analytica is run by Steve Bannon. It is funded by Robert and Rebekah Mercer, and the Cambridge Analytica whistleblower, Christopher Wylie, told me in September 2019 that the parent company, SCL, and Cambridge Analytica used the Philippines 'as a Petri dish' because law and order is weak, they can try things with relative impunity and when a manipulation tactic works, they would 'port it over to the West', to the United States.

When you look at the Cambridge Analytica scandal, the biggest number of compromised accounts, and you're talking roughly 76 million, were in the United States. But the country that had the second highest number of compromised Facebook accounts was the Philippines.

Andrew Keen: Maria, you started up in traditional media and television and then you became a start-up entrepreneur yourself, founding Rappler. Do you feel as if in all this experience they've taken away the internet from you, that the original ideals of the digital revolution have been profoundly corrupted?

Maria Ressa: It's a perversion of what it was supposed to be. It's baked into Rappler that we build communities of action and the food we feed communities is journalism. I had hoped that we could help build institutions bottom-up, and it gave a mission to journalism that I didn't feel when I was working for an American network.

The kind of manipulation that came from Russian disinformation, the idea is not to make a candidate win or lose; it's to make the population lose trust in anything. And when they don't trust anything, where there's no credibility of institutions, then the voice with the loudest megaphone wins. And so in a situation like that, you rob the people. The way we've seen it work in the Philippines now is that a lie is when you say a lie a million times it becomes a fact, except it's a lie. So without facts, you don't have truth, and without truth you can't have trust. That means you don't have democracy.

Andrew Keen: But this isn't the twentieth-century version of totalitarianism. It's not Orwell, is it? It's not *1984*; in *1984* there was a single truth, a single voice.

Maria Ressa: This is chaos.

Andrew Keen: Informational chaos. They flood the market with data, with lies.

Maria Ressa: Democracy is based on us being able to make a choice, and you can't make a choice if you don't know what's real and what's an illusion, what's fact and what's fiction. And that's the kind of weaponization of social media that's happened. Propaganda has been there forever, but propaganda said a million times now replaces facts.

So we do have alternative realities, and this goes back to the way the internet is also set up. We have different feeds. Why is my reality more important than your reality? Before the tech platforms became the world's largest distributor of news, journalist organizations were in charge of both distribution and gate-keeping facts, making sure that the public sphere is not polluted. That's all gone now, and that's part of the reason that democracy as we know it has gone.

We need to do something substantive and it goes back to the social media giants, to these tech platforms. What can they do to make sure that this virus of lies actually stops?

Andrew Keen: So what you've called the virus of lies, how can it be confronted? What are the most effective ways to turn this thing around?

Maria Ressa: In the short term, the tech platforms are the only ones who can take action. We can wait for government regulation, but that will take time. And part of the reason we work with all the tech platforms is precisely because in our case, it's here and now. If nothing significant is done, this has a direct impact not just on Rappler, but on my future. Everything I've built in my career is on the line now, and what this lack of gate-keeping has done is make the fabric of our society very weak because it sells the choice to the highest bidder. Do you agree with me on this?

Andrew Keen: Well, you're the authority – you're living on the front line of this.

Maria Ressa: But the way the advertising, the micro-targeting, is done subverts choice.

Andrew Keen: So it's the business model of the Facebooks and the Googles of the world?

Maria Ressa: Yes. It's the social media platforms because it pushes you to extremes, right. It empties the center, because to keep you on the platform they need to keep feeding you more and more extreme views of the view you're already leaning toward.

Andrew Keen: So it's compounding echo chambers, in every sense?

Maria Ressa: And it's tearing us further apart. So if you lean right, you get pushed further right. If you lean left, you get pushed further left. What happens to the middle?

Andrew Keen: And meanwhile Facebook makes billions of dollars out of all of this.

Maria Ressa: And that's part of what needs to change. So David Kaye, the UN Special Rapporteur on the Promotion and Protection of the Right to Freedom of Opinion and Expression, suggested that something like content moderation, which is what we would call 'gate-keeping', be based on the UN Declaration of Human Rights. Because what's happened is that these attacks literally change people's minds. It's like Nazi Germany. In my case, the government has decided they're going to try to replace the description that people associate with me, 'journalist', with 'criminal'. And they say it in social media and then it comes out of the mouth of President Duterte, and of government officials. When you do that, you've changed reality. And people like me, the people on the front lines, have no recourse.

Andrew Keen: So are you saying that social media companies need to become curators, more like traditional media companies?

Maria Ressa: Social media companies have to be held accountable for the damage that is done on their platforms, the same way that newsgroups are held liable for the lies.

Andrew Keen: How is that going to work though? Should we perhaps begin, at least in the United States, by taking away safe harbor from them?

Maria Ressa: I think the way the law has allowed the social media platforms to behave has led to the deterioration of democracy everywhere. So the first thing is, why not demand like a driver's license?

Andrew Keen: You mean driver's license in terms of doing away with anonymity, so you have to show whom you are able to post?

Maria Ressa: Facebook says that it does not condone fake accounts, and yet there are millions of fake accounts and they take them down all the time. Just today they announced that they were taking down third-party groups who had access to the data that they had. These fake accounts in the disclosure, a few years ago they said that they had a higher than average number of fake accounts in the Philippines, so the first thing is to make them stick to the rules that they actually say.

The second is the assumptions that engineers have made about content moderation. The Napalm girl, an iconic photo by Nick Ut of the girl running away in Vietnam, was taken down by a content moderator in Manila, who took it down based on a checklist that said 'Naked – out'. No context, nothing.

Andrew Keen: But to do these things, Facebook has to undermine their own revenue. Are they willing to do that, or does it require government intervention?

Maria Ressa: I think it's both. I think it's enlightened self-interest, because they don't want to create a world where they cannot exist. And then the second thing is to work against their own revenue model – that's a massive change and it's a lot of money that could be lost. Government regulation could kick in, but I worry that you throw the baby out with the bathwater, both on free speech and in terms of the potential for this technology to do good. We still work with Facebook – we're one of their two Filipino fact-checking partners, because I saw its ability to build these communities of action. We grew 100 to 300 per cent, year on year, our first few years until 2015.

I think it can still be done but not when the platforms allow this incitement to hate, this kind of manipulation that subverts choice.

Andrew Keen: Is the European model the one that you think has the best chance of taking on the tech giants – a more regulatory approach – or do you think that is also somehow flawed?

Maria Ressa: It's flawed because it isn't a one-size-fits-all answer, and this is going to be a problem for the tech giants. At one level you have one platform where, if you put Facebook and WhatsApp together, you're connecting 2.7 billion people around the world. We've never had that many people on one platform, because every country used to have its own vertical media.

So there's this huge potential. At the same time, if you don't stop the lies, a lie in the United States travels to the Philippines, and vice versa – and that's what is tainting this entire ecosystem. So I don't know if GDPR is the right model – it seems simplistic to me. But I've testified in Ottawa, where the Members of Parliament of fourteen nations have come together, led by Canada. They've asked sophisticated questions and they're looking for answers, and in the end I think the solution to this is transparency. So far, the platforms have taken down millions of accounts globally, but while Twitter releases all the data, Facebook doesn't really, and Google certainly doesn't. So what can we do? What if there was a global repository? It is explained to you, so you can see it. And then you can begin to tear down these networks – I call them terrorist networks, because they're spreading lies and they're acting like terrorists in our democracies.

Why can't there be a global Interpol who will prevent the impunity of these information operations? And when they're caught, there are penalties. That's what will stop it.

Andrew Keen: And this is a kind of algorithmic transparency?

Maria Ressa: It's more than an algorithmic transparency – it's the foundation of our methodology. We fact-check a lie, and when we find the lie you can begin to look at the networks that spread that lie. And sooner or later, like terrorist organizations in the real world, you begin to tear them down. And if you do that in a transparent manner and people see that there are costs to doing this, this will stop. So the Mueller Report is very clear about what Russian disinformation did in the 2016 elections. A former KGB agent said that with disinformation, the first time you encounter it, you can move forward and go back to yourself. But if you're fed a diet of this, he compared it to drugs; so the first time you take a drug you're okay, but if you get addicted to this drug it wears down your body and mind. And if you've taken the drug a million times, you're a fundamentally different person.

That's what's happening with these networks of disinformation. It is weakening the body politic. It is weakening and killing democracy.

Andrew Keen: What happens if the lies originate from politicians?

Maria Ressa: Well, that's what we're seeing in many parts of the world. Freedom House said in November 2017 that in at least 28 countries around the world, cheap armies on social media were rolling back democracy. And then in 2018, the Computational Propaganda Research Project at Oxford University said that number was up to 48. I don't know what it is in 2019, but I certainly know in my country that this is state-sponsored. And while the government continues to deny that, when two of the three main content creators were given government posts, you know they're connected. And we've watched this; it's replicated in many other countries around the world.

Andrew Keen: It's one thing to pay for troll farms to lie, but do you think these senior politicians know they're lying, or do they believe what they say?

Maria Ressa: I go back to Cambridge Analytica and you can see in everything that's been exposed there, both the people working in Cambridge Analytica and the people who hire them. In the Philippines, we went and found SCL, the parent company of Cambridge Analytica, and they had a relationship with Duterte. Power and money are coming together and it is a potent combination that if it is not addressed will kill. If no substantive action is taken, democracy as we know it is dead.

RANA FOROOHAR

I've always been a big admirer of Rana Foroohar's columns in the *Financial Times*, in which she expertly dissects the lies and hypocrisy of Wall Street and Silicon Valley, with a sharp wit that makes her writing entertaining as well as important. Her book *Don't Be Evil* is a particularly valuable antidote to the gushing adoration of Silicon Valley that still infects much of the tech press.

I interviewed Rana in a tiny room at the *Financial Times* offices in New York City. It was like a bit of England in high-tech Lower Manhattan, but there was nothing old-fashioned about Rana's conversation, which I hope captures the sharpness of her dissection of the Silicon Valley economy.

Andrew Keen: Rana Foroohar, *Financial Times* columnist, you've become a historian of the platforms and your new book, *Don't Be Evil*, is about the history of the platforms. What have you discovered?

Rana Foroohar: Well, a few things: Silicon Valley, as many people have written, was a very idealistic place for a long time. And the internet itself used to be more of a decentralized platform.

As the Valley grew and became one of the largest economies in the world, there's been a lot of changes culturally and economically; you moved into a system where there were a lot of hippies, to one where it's being mostly run by libertarians, and this is something that always gives me pause. There's kind of a mythology in the US and it's one that's pushed in Washington: 'Oh, the Silicon Valley type: Sheryl Sandberg, Mark Zuckerberg, Eric Schmidt – they're all pushing a liberal agenda.' I don't think they're pushing a liberal agenda at all; I think they're pushing a *libertarian* agenda.

If you look at the leaders in the Valley, they give money to both political parties. They will lobby whoever is in their best interest. And I would argue we haven't had a *mea culpa* for their role in the 2016 election meddling scandal in the US.

And this to me represents where it makes sense that we would be, after 40 years of deregulation: governments doing nothing but cutting taxes, the private sector being left to make its own rules. A company like Facebook is the apex of that: it's what you would imagine would be born of that kind of society. But I think that the pendulum is turning, and I think you see that in our presidential debate around 2020.

Andrew Keen: Isn't that a contradiction, though? You say that Silicon Valley is lacking morality and you've titled your new book *Don't Be Evil*, which I assume is an ironic take on that early Google mantra. But wouldn't it be fair to say that many of the engineers at Google and other people in Silicon Valley did want technology to make the world a better place and believed that it would?

Rana Foroohar: I think that's absolutely true, but I would draw a sharp line with the rank-and-file engineers in these companies, who are beginning to revolt against their own companies. We've seen huge turnover at Facebook. We've seen Google stepping up on everything from not wanting to do a censored search engine in China, to sexism within the company, to the use of Google technologies by the US military. You're seeing real activism amongst the rank and file, which is great, but it's been a relatively short-term phenomenon. And at the top, the leadership is still in Washington, lobbying for the same old 'Don't regulate us, we need to be the national champions against China,' even as they're doing business in the places that their workers are concerned about. And I think that's very problematic.

Andrew Keen: So you believe that Silicon Valley has essentially corrupted capitalism?

Rana Foroohar: Well, I think capitalism was already doing a pretty good job of being corrupted. As I say, my last book was about Wall Street, but I see a lot of parallels. I look at the Valley and at the business model of platform firms very much like I look at the business model of the largest banks: these companies both create a marketplace and play in the marketplace. They're incredibly opaque; they have incredible information and advantages over other players, and that skews the economy.

I joined the *FT* about two years ago and my mandate was to cover the biggest economic and business stories in global markets, and so I began to follow the money. I discovered 80 per cent of corporate value was in 10 per cent of IP-rich companies, many of them in the Valley.

At the same time, two things happened. A number of companies in different spaces kept coming to me and saying, 'We're being squashed by these large players. They have incredible legal might. They have incredible lobbying might and they've captured Washington.' And that was very similar to what I heard in the 2008 financial crisis.

Andrew Keen: So the platforms have had a bad impact on capitalism, even if they haven't ruined it, because it was perhaps originally ruined by the banks. But what about democracy? Is there a relationship between the large players in Silicon Valley and democracy?

Rana Foroohar: I think there is and I think that the link is the sense that most Americans have that the economy is rigged. They believe the economy is controlled by large moneyed interests, a handful of companies, a handful of titans.

Andrew Keen: And that's what you're saying as well?

Rana Foroohar: It's what I'm saying as well.

Andrew Keen: So what's the impact on democracy? Because the original idea was that Google would give out all this information, or at least create links to the information on the internet. Everyone would have access to it and everyone would be able to make more coherent, responsible choices when it comes to politics and elections. Hasn't that happened?

Rana Foroohar: No, it patently hasn't happened, and we can see any number of ways in which platform technologies, simply by the nature of the business model, have been used to do everything from push genocide in Myanmar to tip the scales in elections in the US and Europe.

So, no, I don't think they've helped liberal democracy. I don't think Larry and Sergey and Marissa Mayer were trying to do anything nefarious when they were originally developing these companies, but I think that there was a naivety and a sense of doing God's work, a sense that 'we know best' that I keep finding, which is amazing to me.

Andrew Keen: Are you suggesting that the business model of the dominant platforms, not Apple but Google and Facebook, the model where we get the search engines and the social networks for free and we essentially pay with our data – are you saying *that* business model by definition undermines democracy?

Rana Foroohar: I am, in two ways: first of all, if you look at the undermining of capitalism and growing inequality in rich companies, I would say that the model of targeted advertising fuels that because you are taking what is the new oil data and you are harvesting it, you are not telling people what it's worth and the company is taking the vast majority of the wealth. There are academics looking now, even within the structure of the University of Chicago model of anti-trust, to show, 'Hey, these companies have been growing their average revenue per user exponentially over the last decades but our service offerings haven't really improved that much.'

So there's a huge amount of value that's going directly to the companies. Maybe some of it should be going to consumers, and that's what states like California I think are trying to get at with some of their new regulatory proposals.

Andrew Keen: So what are we going to do about all this? You've been a leading advocate on regulation, and perhaps even breaking up some of the platforms.

Rana Foroohar: Well, I've never believed that self-regulation worked. I had a conversation with Roger McNamee two years ago. He came into my office and we started talking about his ideas and I remember we talked about this whole thing, and I said, 'It's going to have to be regulation,' and he said, 'No, I don't think we should jump to that yet. We should give them a chance.'

Well, self-regulation has not worked, and governments are going to have to step in. We're going to have to figure out what we want the internet to be, whom we want it to serve, and how we're going to divide up this very rich pie, and that's going to be a robust discussion.

Andrew Keen: Who are 'we', Rana?

Rana Foroohar: Citizens, not consumers, and I think that's a word that I'd like to start hearing a lot more of.

Andrew Keen: Is there such a thing as a US citizen?

Rana Foroohar: Yes, absolutely there is. You and I are citizens. People like Alexandria Ocasio-Cortez are making this point. Elizabeth Warren is making this point. I think you're going to see the problem of oligopoly, of which Silicon Valley is at the apex, and the fact that we've become a consumer society as part of the problem. We need to go back to being a society of citizens who make choices about economic ecosystems that are in our interest as a whole.

Andrew Keen: So if Donald Trump was here, and fortunately he isn't, he would say, 'Oh, just another socialist.' It's ironic that we're at the home of the *Financial Times*, the leading newspaper about global capitalism, but can one regulate and maintain capitalism?

Rana Foroohar: Absolutely you can. Adam Smith would have said that the three things that you need for healthy capitalism are transparency in markets, equal access to data, and a shared moral framework. And I would say that we have none of those things right now. And I would also say to Donald Trump, 'Guess what? Seventy per cent of millennial voters, which is now the largest voting bloc, don't mind the word socialist.'

Andrew Keen: So what to do? Should Google and Facebook be broken up? Are they by definition monopolists and do we need to reinvigorate the anti-trust?

Rana Foroohar: Yes, I think we do. I think there's a rich debate in anti-trust going on right now. There are some who believe that we can use the existing Chicago School principles to simply show that data has value, and then you can come up with mathematical models to show that there actually has been monopoly power taken by these companies. That's one approach.

There's another approach using the kind of New Brandeis School, which is about power; it's about saying, 'Look, these companies are like railroads. They can simply buy politicians. They can simply make their own rules. They have too much power and you need to break them up for that purpose.'

I take a third angle on this, and it's maybe similar to the way Elizabeth Warren looks at it, which is that I see them like big holding banks. I think it's unfair to both *be* the market and *play* in the market. And so certain tweaks have to be made to that rule, just as there have been in banking, in order to make the marketplace fair and more competitive.

Andrew Keen: Should we simply in the US copy what's happening in Europe? Is Vestager the pioneer of all this?

Rana Foroohar: Vestager is great in terms of speaking truth to power, but I'd argue that some of the California privacy regulations and some of the data proposals that are upcoming in California are even maybe tougher than GDPR. What I like about these is that by forcing more disclosure in a clear way about what consumers are actually signing over, that kind of transparency is very important because then people can make an informed market choice.

It also starts a debate about the extent of surveillance, which we didn't even have because we didn't know. And I don't think the platform firms are the only ones that are going to be talking about this. If you look at the new proposals about a data dividend, which Governor Newsom has talked about, this would be paid out potentially by any company that was collecting personal data. Now that's not just the platform companies: it could be an auto firm, it could be Starbucks...

Andrew Keen: What does that mean, a data dividend?

Rana Foroohar: The idea is that all our personal data has value and it's an asset that should be marked on a balance sheet. You and I should be able to own some of that value. Some people like Glen Weyl, the economist who wrote a wonderful book called *Radical Markets*, feel that it should be counted as labor, and so we should actually get paid for our data. The point is that some of the wealth should be flowing not just toward the companies, but toward the people who are giving the data.

There's a precedent for this if you think about it: citizens in Alaska and in Norway that live in commodities-rich countries get payouts for those resources in the form of sovereign wealth funds or in the form of yearly checks, and so it would be very similar to that.

Andrew Keen: Are we seeing a wave of new start-ups focusing on this issue? Are we going to see the anti-Google emerge, or the anti-Facebook?

Rana Foroohar: I think you will, and I think you already would have if the markets weren't so dominated right now. I was at a dinner party with a three-time entrepreneur in New England and we were talking about how hard it is to come up against the platform giants. He told me that he'd been trying to sell his most recent company, a data analysis firm, to Facebook and he had made some of the code open-source so they could work with it, and they were also looking at another firm and they had an internal project going on.

In the end, they decided to go with their own internal project, but he felt that they'd taken some of his source code ideas and he went to complain about this and said, 'Look, I can't fight you legally, but I think this is wrong and I want you to know it.' And his contact there said, 'Well look, you have to understand that we're working with six times as much data per second as the largest banks, but we're making one hundred thousandth the amount of profit on it. If we have to pay for everything, we don't have a business model.' I find that a very telling quote. I think that what this says is that these companies are getting a lot of inputs for free, and that's one of the reasons they have 43 per cent profit margins.

Andrew Keen: You've talked a lot about Facebook and Google, and you've mentioned Apple, but you haven't talked about the biggest platform of them all – Amazon, who have a different business model. Are you as fearful of them? Do they need to be broken up, too?

Rana Foroohar: I think they need to have the same rules that Warren is proposing that would hit Google and Facebook, which are if you're an over $25 billion company and you're both creating and playing in a market, you need to be regulated in such a way that you don't have unfair control. And that's just basic: you can't be a bank and trade aluminum and own all the aluminum in the world – there are rules around that, though they aren't always enforced.

And I think that's what we need there. I think that Amazon has incredible asymmetry in its transactions, incredible advantages, and I think the fact that it was allowed to go around and scoop up information in the course of its city search that it can now use with impunity should have been illegal.

Andrew Keen: Let's end on a Silicon Valley note, and let's try to be a bit more positive.

Let's say some of the stuff that you're suggesting happens and that the monopolies are broken up. Let's say we have the rise of innovative companies built around data, and let's say some of that data revenue flows back to people. Let's say that the information economy becomes less of an echo chamber and more open. How can that enrich democracy? Because democracy as I think everyone would acknowledge, is in crisis at the moment, particularly in the West. If some of the reforms that you're championing happen, maybe under President Warren or President Biden, how will democracy be improved?

Rana Foroohar: Well, I think that if you have a more robust economic ecosystem where more people are able to pursue the American dream, to move up the ladder, to start businesses, to not feel as though their prospects are hindered, and to not see their children less well off than they are, of course that helps liberal democracy.

The crisis in liberal democracy came to a head with the financial crisis, after which it became clear that our government was favoring larger, richer players over smaller individuals, Wall Street over homeowners – that was part of a 40-year crisis in which you had a growing inequality, and that's part of oligopoly and the concentration of power. And if you can get at those things, I think you can fix liberal democracy.

PART 2

WAKING UP
FROM UTOPIA

DAVID KIRKPATRICK

David Kirkpatrick and I haven't always agreed about the digital revolution, and particularly regarding the role of social media in the supposed democratization of society. There was a time a few years ago when he probably thought of me as a bit of a 'yesterday' – somebody too nostalgic for the certainties of the twentieth-century analog age. And while I've always respected the fluency of his writing and the intellectual heft of his Techonomy conferences, I have to admit that I sometimes thought his optimistic embrace of social media, particularly in his 2010 book *The Facebook Effect,* was a little too 'tomorrow'.

However, what I respect most about David is his willingness to publicly change his mind. As one of the world's leading authorities on Facebook, he has dramatically shifted his opinion on the company over the last few years, going from an enthusiast to an outspoken critic. As Keynes famously said, 'When the facts change, I change my mind,' and as you can tell from this conversation with David, in the wake of recent Facebook scandals, he has sharply changed *his* mind, giving his opinions credibility and relevance.

Andrew Keen: David Kirkpatrick, you are perhaps the world's leading authority on Facebook and wrote the bible on Facebook, *The Facebook Effect*, in 2010, but since then you've dramatically changed your mind on Facebook, and today you're much more critical and pessimistic. Do you feel personally let down by Facebook, about their potential to remake the world, and particularly democracy?

David Kirkpatrick: Well, I feel very disappointed that they failed to anticipate the harm that their service could cause alongside the virtues that it brought to the world, and so in that sense I do feel let down. But with Facebook it's not by a company, it's by a person. This is a company that is a unilateral dictatorship and Mark Zuckerberg is the decision maker, and he chose not to prioritize the issues of potential harm and instead to go for growth at all costs. And that is the single biggest reason why we find ourselves with so many things going wrong.

Andrew Keen: That's an interesting response, David. Sheryl Sandberg doesn't matter; everything at Facebook is all about Zuckerberg?

David Kirkpatrick: Well, Sheryl Sandberg doesn't control the company – she works for him. She does matter, and I think she's made errors, too. I respect them both in many ways, and I try not to make *ad hominem* attacks on them, although the problems that their service has caused the world are so severe that it's hard not to be deeply disappointed in them as people.

Andrew Keen: That's a pretty radical thing to say – explain that.

David Kirkpatrick: Well, let me explain what I was going to say about Sheryl. Mark told me when I was writing my book that he hired her partly because of her government experience and running Facebook was going to be increasingly like running a government. But ironically that is not what she did.

Instead of bringing her government experience to bear and trying to implement governance-like reforms and structures inside the system, she built one of the best businesses that has ever been built, in a generally heedless manner. They could have built a good ad business with a lot more controls and protective features and probably not been as profitable as they are, but I believe it would have worked. And they wouldn't have grown as quickly, but they chose to grow at all costs.

The irony is that he said she had government experience and Facebook was going to be like a government, but she has not functioned as a government figure inside the company – she's functioned as a cheerleader for a purely exploitative capitalist business model.

Andrew Keen: So is Facebook the epitome of what Shoshana Zuboff called 'surveillance capitalism'? Is that the best summary of the model, and is that essentially what's gone wrong with the company?

David Kirkpatrick: I don't think Facebook is the only example of surveillance capitalism. Surveillance capitalism is a macro-phenomenon that goes well beyond Facebook and extends to the camera-based society, YouTube, Google, all these messaging services, particularly in China, and there's plenty of other ways that surveillance capitalism is harming the world and impairing our freedom of action.

Rather than thinking of surveillance capitalism, I am more along the lines of Kristin Harris's analysis in which she talks about the predatory database advertising model, which is attention-based and depends on disrupting the user's life in order to profit for the vendor, the advertising platform. However, Kristin doesn't have a simple answer. Roger McNamee tends to have a somewhat simpler answer, which is that they shouldn't be allowed to use that business model. This strikes me as impractical because I just don't see how you get from here to there.

The surveillance part is a big part of it, but it's not just that they're surveilling us; it's that they're surveilling us for their own profit, and therefore have no incentive to stop surveilling us.

Andrew Keen: Zuboff suggests that it was Sandberg who imported the surveillance capitalist business model from

Google to Facebook, and I think McNamee also agrees with that.

David Kirkpatrick: I wouldn't disagree with that.

Andrew Keen: So why is Zuckerberg so important, if Sandberg is the pioneer of this corrosive business model?

David Kirkpatrick: Look, I blame Sheryl Sandberg for bringing that business model in and not stopping to think about some of the consequences. I do think both of them have got drunk on the money, but it is technically accurate that before Sheryl arrived there was in effect no business model. After she arrived they sat around, and she would write on a whiteboard, 'What business are we in?' They didn't even know what business they were in. They didn't know how they were going to make money. That had not been Mark's priority and Sheryl figured it out in a way that was enormously profitable, and she executed it with some strategic brilliance, without considering the consequences on society.

Yes, she brought a targeted ad-based business model with her from Google, and that's what they used.

Andrew Keen: David, in *The Facebook Effect* your presentation of Facebook was as a kind of engine of democracy. Did you have a moment over the last eight years where you recognized that Facebook wasn't this engine of democracy?

David Kirkpatrick: Well, when I was interviewing Mark Zuckerberg on stage at Techonomy two days after the election and he said it was a crazy idea that fake news on Facebook affected the election of Donald Trump, that was a revelatory moment for me. Processing it in subsequent weeks and the world's reaction to it was a pretty big force on my thinking, although I had already been quite concerned prior to that about how worried I was about the sheer power these companies were gaining with governments. But I wouldn't entirely agree with your formulation because the way I talked about it in my book was not exactly as a force for democracy, but a force for the empowerment of the individual. That is the distinction; it can translate into being a force for democracy and it often has and I think it still does in many ways. The problem is that it is also a force for anti-democracy – it depends on what the empowered individuals are trying to accomplish.

If the empowered individuals are trying to work for the election of Barack Obama or the promotion of the MeToo Movement or any other thing that we might consider socially admirable or progressive, it does work in those contexts. So it still has that quality, but it also has the quality that when people who have evil and malicious intent want to abuse the system, it unfortunately lends itself very readily to that abuse, which is why we get Orbán, Duterte, Bolsonaro, etcetera, etcetera. I think that one of the main reasons those figures have become such major forces on the world's stage is that they are all masters of abusing social media and in particular Facebook, because the rules don't prevent them from doing so.

Andrew Keen: So you're suggesting that the Bolsonaros and the Erdogans and the Dutertes of the world are cheats and that they're abusing Facebook; they're not using it legitimately?

David Kirkpatrick: Every one of those is a cheat and an abuser of Facebook, absolutely unequivocally; that is well known. There's plenty of evidence in each of those cases, and it's also true for the anti-democratic forces that are on the rise in Poland. It's true in many other countries in Eastern Europe, in the Orbán orbit. It's true in many countries of the world, including Vietnam and elsewhere; and the best example ultimately is Myanmar, where the military junta used it to perpetrate genocide with fake news and incendiary speech that was intended to rouse people toward violence.

You can't really rouse people toward violence by using the system honestly, in most cases. In Myanmar, in Sri Lanka, in the Philippines, just to take Southeast Asia, it's very easy to concoct sensational messages that are inaccurate or dishonest, that aim to inspire people to hate someone that is politically advantageous for the person doing the manipulating.

One good example is the way that Duterte continues to target Maria Ressa, the famous and brave journalist in the Philippines.

He has an entire team of probably thousands of people who use social media to stir up trouble day in and day out. This is true in India, too; the party in power in India have employed thousands of people who create whatever incendiary message they can to achieve their political goals, which is often to rouse people to fear and anger, in order to support their political interests. Fear and anger when it's invoked leads people to support autocrats; that's like the simple formula, and it works. And you can generate fear and anger with fake messages in Facebook.

Andrew Keen: David, was this model pioneered by Putin in Russia? Was Putin the first politician who got it?

David Kirkpatrick: Putin has been using this kind of system to manipulate the Russian population for decades – he wasn't doing it first in Facebook. I think that when he succeeded in doing it in order to help Donald Trump get elected, it led to a series of revelations for other political leaders around the world of what was possible.

In that sense, he was the teacher. Unfortunately, the controversy that surrounded Cambridge Analytica and the Russian manipulation inside Facebook during the campaign in 2016, the coverage that got globally, was revelatory to politicians in many countries. And it didn't teach them that you shouldn't do it; it taught them that you could and therefore, from their standpoint, should do it.

Andrew Keen: So David, how do we fix this? If Mark Zuckerberg or Sheryl Sandberg were to take a call from you, what would you tell them to do?

David Kirkpatrick: It is fixable, but it's not fixable while maintaining a company with 40 per cent plus net margins, which is what Facebook has. Facebook on a per dollar of revenue basis is the most profitable large company that has ever existed. That is not an overstatement. Facebook has after-tax profit margins in the vicinity of 40 per cent. Google's net margins are in the 25 per cent and below range. Before Facebook started doing any remediation, they routinely had net after-tax margins of 43 to 45 per cent, which means for every dollar of revenue, after they paid for everything it took to run the system, they kept 45 cents. That is unbelievable profitability, so you can't maintain that and fix the system.

By the way, before we go back to the remediation, my fundamental criticism of Zuckerberg and Sandberg is they prioritize making that much money. The biggest lie that they promulgate is that they don't try to make so much money. If you listen to the interview that was done at the Code Conference by Casey Newton, they are both reiterating it: 'We're not rapacious capitalists. We don't think about making money.' It's such disingenuous rhetoric to say, 'We aren't trying to make tons of money,' when they're the most profitable company of their scale that's ever existed. It's insulting to every other business to say they're not trying hard to make money, because they're doing it better than anybody else. And they also keep saying, 'We were too slow to see all these harms coming.' The reason they were too slow was that they were drunk on the wealth they were generating and the stock appreciation they were individually benefiting from.

Andrew Keen: So do they know they're lying, or are they deluding themselves?

David Kirkpatrick: They're deluding themselves. They think we don't appreciate all the good things that Facebook brings to the world and that the world is unfair in our criticism of them because we are only focusing on the negative. The positive overwhelmingly outweighs the negative, but we don't see that because the negative is more sensational.

They say, 'Yes, we were slow and yes, we needed to do more and yes, we made a lot of mistakes.' In fact, in that interview at the Code Conference, I think Bosworth says they were Pollyannaish until last year. But they were worse than Pollyannaish – they were willfully ignorant of the potential negatives because they were so eager to keep growing and making money.

There's an element of them thinking that if they didn't grow fast, somebody else would eat their lunch. I understand that, but they should have been willing to tolerate that risk in order not to create all these harms that they've engendered.

Andrew Keen: So has the time come for the regulators to step in? It sounds to me, at least in your presentation, that these people are congenital liars.

David Kirkpatrick: I didn't say they were congenital liars; I said they were self-delusional. To say they're congenital liars would be to presume that they're willfully lying. I do think willful lies do emerge, but I don't think of them as congenital liars. I think their delusions can be traced back to their wealth. If you look at Zuckerberg, the richest 35-year-old in human history, it's pretty easy to think, 'If I'm this rich I must be smarter than everybody else and they just don't get it. And I'm entitled to keep doing what I'm doing. And anyway, I'm going to give it away and cure all diseases, so I deserve the money.' I think that kind of wealth makes it very hard for people to step back and make a rational assessment of the impact of their behavior.

I'm not saying I know how to regulate it, but I will guarantee you regulation is coming.

All across the world the governments are stepping up; they are not going to sit back anymore. If you look, for example, at the Democratic presidential candidates, every single one of them has a position on the regulation of social media and the majority of them say yes when asked whether these services should be broken up. That is a major sea change that's really only happened in the last six to nine months.

Andrew Keen: As you said, Facebook is the most profitable company in history. Couldn't they just employ armies of curators to make sure that the Dutertes and Bolsonaros and Putins of the world don't cheat the system?

David Kirkpatrick: I think in some sense that's what they have to do and they are starting to do that. They brag about the 30,000 curators they have now and Casey Newton at *The Verge* has done these extraordinary articles about the suffering those people encounter, looking at all these suicides and sexual depravity and child pornography, all the awful stuff that they have to look at, day in and day out. And there aren't nearly enough of them, but unfortunately, even if they were to employ hundreds of thousands, it would not be completely sufficient.

I believe they are a media company and that they bear responsibility for the content that runs on their services. They've acknowledged this in some ways but they continue to deny the idea that they should be considered a media company. And if you accept that, it does imply enormous additional expense in order to monitor the content and to take a lot more stuff down, to be much more vigilant; they can employ software so it's not just a bodies issue, but it will be enormously costly. And it should be, because the world's safety and the future of social harmony in some ways depends on it. This is the town square of the planet – they are controlling speech for a large portion of the planet, and whatever it costs, they should spend the money to do that responsibly.

DOUGLAS RUSHKOFF

Of all the people interviewed in this book, I think Doug Rushkoff is the most nostalgic for a previous time in history. But in contrast with the Putins and Trumps of the world, with their dishonest fetishization of nationalism, Doug's nostalgia is for a simpler period in history, a time before global surveillance capitalism and all it has brought with it. So Doug is a good 'yesterday' who genuinely wants to make the world a fairer place.

Of all my subjects, I think Doug is the thinker who is most simultaneously a 'tomorrow' *and* a 'yesterday'. On the one hand, he is one of the world's leading tech writers and thinkers; on the other, he is a scholar of a pre-capitalist past which he thinks can be recaptured in the twenty-first century. But most of all, as you can tell from this interview, he is an inspiring conversationalist whose views are defiantly independent and who can't be pigeonholed into any single ideological box.

Andrew Keen: Douglas Rushkoff, the author of *Team Human* and also of many other books and acclaimed technologist, tell me a little bit about yourself; how would you summarize your achievements?

Douglas Rushkoff: I guess the main thing I've been doing in my professional life has been fighting over the set and setting of digital technology. I was very enthusiastic about the potential of this stuff to unleash a dormant capacity of human beings to collaborate and cooperate in ways that we hadn't yet imagined, that it would be as big as the invention of language or text in allowing for new forms of communication and working together.

I feel like I've been fighting against what turns out to be corporate capitalism, fighting against the idea that the internet is here to figure out ways to extract more money and data from people and to support these exponential business plans. I'm from the early cyberpunk, psychedelic pro-human technology culture and I watched it get overrun by the *Wired* magazine business culture, and I'm still here writing books and doing talks and making podcasts and movies that are looking at how we retain or even enhance human autonomy, in spite of all this.

Andrew Keen: Well, I'm thrilled you're still around. You've got this new book *Team Human* which came out of a podcast.

The reason I asked that question is I'm guessing that your self-definition and your definition of what it means to be human are kind of the same. In other words, do you see yourself and your goals in your life as a manifestation of a certain kind of humanness?

Douglas Rushkoff: Certainly in intent, if not in result. I'm probably as much a victim and perpetrator of the things I'm railing against as anybody else. I have my 401k plan and I have an automobile and I'm not living a totally human life that I would aspire to, but I'm a lateral thinker and I'm someone who looks at patterns in new ways and tries to feel connected to other people rather than automated. I value my very local existence, my eye contact with other people, and that on-the-ground scaled human reality.

Andrew Keen: So you juxtaposed yourself or your lifestyle with the corporates, with the *Wired* magazine, with the titans of Silicon Valley. Are you suggesting that those people on the other side are not really human?

Douglas Rushkoff: They're definitely human. They've just succumbed to really dehumanizing models of the world. They've accepted corporate capitalism as a fact of nature. They really believe that Darwin wrote a book about evolution that says that individuals compete for survival against one another, and they think that's the science.

And they think the market is somehow a natural expression of that. They don't know that Darwin said the opposite; that evolution is actually the story of how species collaborate and cooperate, amongst themselves and with other species, in order to ensure mutual survival. And they don't know that the market ideology that they are so committed to, this idea that the economy has to grow in order for everything to be okay, is just an artifact of a very particular economic operating system that was put in place in the twelfth and thirteenth centuries by monarchs trying to stem the rise of the middle class and we've accepted it at face value.

So no, they're not inhuman; they're definitely human beings. They've just been as hypnotized by the rules of corporate capitalism as their users are by the interfaces and all the mean tricks that they put into our news feeds and apps to addict us or to trigger our brain stem into fight or flight. They're still human; they're just human beings acting in the silliest, most frightened ways.

Andrew Keen: So, tie in your notion of what it means to be human and what it means to be part of *Team Human* with democracy. Because when I read your book and when I listen to your speeches and your podcasts, it seems to me that *Team Human* is all about a kind of ideal form of democracy – is that fair?

Douglas Rushkoff: I would say so. *Team Human* is written for a society that needs a lot of remedial help. If I don't talk so much about solidarity it's because I'm talking so much about rapport, which is a prerequisite for solidarity.

Andrew Keen: What do you mean by that word, rapport?

Douglas Rushkoff: You need to be able to look in someone's eyes and connect with another human being. The trick for labor and democracy in the age of Uber and Amazon Turk is that unlike the industrial age, you're not standing on the assembly line next to another person. You can't talk to your co-workers at lunch when you eat lunch in the coalmine and say, 'Hey buddy, this kind of stinks doesn't it? They're not paying us enough.' You can't forge solidarity if you don't have the ability to establish basic rapport. And rapport is the kind of stuff that it's really hard to forge on digital platforms.

Andrew Keen: To be fair, you brought up Uber and this week in San Francisco, Uber drivers went on strike, so there is some rapport in the digital economy, isn't there?

Douglas Rushkoff: Right; it's tremendous that they've been able to do that because there's no chat function on Uber. They're not letting the drivers find one another. There's no community, so they have to form it themselves. And it tends to happen on a local more than a national level. So when I look at the future of democracy, I'm encouraging people to get involved in local politics, where the issues are not so ideological and so easily framed by Twitter or Facebook or stories. A lot of people spend a lot of their time worrying about and voting based on issues that they have no connection to whatsoever. If they were voting and participating more locally and thinking, 'Well, what is the stream where I live? What about the factory in our town? What about our schools?'

Democracy to me looks like joining your local school board, joining your local land zoning board – there's plenty to do. Those rooms are empty and there's usually just a couple of crazy people sitting in the back because they've got nothing better to do.

Andrew Keen: I respect what you're saying, but isn't the reason that these rooms are empty because around the world, not just in the United States but in Brazil and the Philippines, in Turkey and Hungary and Poland and Italy, people want the strong leader. They want an Erdogan. They want a Trump. They want a Bolsonaro. They want a Duterte. And they're voting for them. How do you explain that in your theory of *Team Human*? Have we gone that wrong? Is it a reversion to a dependency on a father figure?

Douglas Rushkoff: Partly. We have a multi-trillion-dollar industry, meaning a technology industry, that is focused primarily on putting people into a fight or flight condition. That's what Facebook does; that's what Twitter is doing. They're all getting us not just to communicate to our amygdala, but to keep us in a state of anxiety and panic, to keep us anti-social so we're depending on technologies for a sense of comfort rather than one another. And when people are in that state, they feel that their very survival is at stake, that brown people are coming over the border, that gypsies are going to kidnap their children, that Mexicans are going to take their jobs, and that everybody is a threat, whether it's the brown people or the Trump people. Everybody feels so threatened that yes, they're going to revert to a childlike state and transfer parental authority onto some leader. This is what I was writing about in 1999, in a book called *Coercion*. I was saying that if we take the tools of traditional advertising, and I meant what the Toyota salesman does to you in the showroom, what the neurolinguistics programming people are doing in sales, the way advertising works, creating a sense of insecurity in the consumer, and then bringing them the answer. If we port those techniques into digital technology, we're going to end up with a very frightened, disoriented public that's going to be incapable of acting like a body politic.

And that's kind of where we are today, so if we want to have people voting intelligently we need to start at the very beginning and help people develop basic coherence, the ability to observe reality around them accurately, and to learn how to engage with other people and not be threatened by other social contact. We're not moving in that direction right now and that's kind of why I had to write that book to say, 'Look; evolution is the story of cooperation and collaboration. Other people are not your enemies; they're your friends. The way to build a strong economy is by everybody mutually getting one another rich, not taking stuff from each other. And the way to organize is not to see the other as some enemy, but to learn to see the human being in the person that you're considering the other.'

Andrew Keen: Ian Bremmer, who I'm sure you know, was on the show last week, and I asked him about fixing democracy – what we need to do, and he said to begin we need to start talking to people who disagree with us. Would you agree with him on that? Or where do we begin to claw back the renaissance?

Douglas Rushkoff: That's one of the first things I say. There's a chapter in *Team Human* called 'Organize', and it's largely about that. It's learning to see the other as a collaborator, in a good way rather than as some kind of enemy. And it's also the willingness to stand up and say, 'Here I am.' That's the hard part – it's embarrassing for people to stand up, but I think I would say the first step almost always happens at the local level. I get so many emails from people who want to restore or retrieve democracy by creating a website that's going to aggregate all the great apps that help democracy. I get that sort of techno-solutionist urge – it's from a beautiful place. They feel like they understand the common thread and they want to just put it all together so people then will have the information they need. And that's not really it.

Andrew Keen: Well, you've been there, right? That's where you were in 1980 or 1985?

Douglas Rushkoff: Well, I didn't think we would build a tool to do it. In 1992 and 1993 when I was talking about the internet as a renaissance, I was saying, 'The internet will give people the confidence they need to go and meet people in real life.' I always believed it was that; we had these great conversations on the WELL and in USENET, and in all these places where I could test out ideas and find out that I'm not crazy and that there were smart people who agreed with me and have extended these arguments. I've always felt about it that way, not that it would be this end in itself, which it's turned into.

But I always tell these folks who want to just build that platform and make this thing or do that new voting thing or the new 'We're going to put democracy on the blockchain' or whatever it is, that what we need first is functional, coherent, grounded, social human beings. If you don't have a basic social fabric, there's no way to vote or to participate out of something other than fear, and that just exacerbates our problems.

Andrew Keen: One of the other themes that have come out in this series of interviews is the need to regulate big tech. Is that also essential? If not to shut them down or break them up, do we need more aggressive regulation of the Facebooks and the Googles of the world if we're going to save democracy?

Douglas Rushkoff: I would say yes and no. Regulation is not my expertise, though it sounds good to me. I always think back to the way I blindly accepted John Barlow's *Declaration of Independence of Cyberspace* which pretty much argued, 'Government, get off the net; we got this one.' And I didn't realize at the time that if you get rid of government you'll give corporations free rein and it's like getting rid of fungus; the bacteria is going to grow.

So I want government back; my problem with regulation is that my experience of it so far are examples like when there was lead in the red paint on Mattel's 'Dora the Explorer' toys back in the 1990s. And everyone was up in arms: 'Oh my God; we've got to regulate the toy industry.' So the toy industry sends the biggest players to meet with the government and come up with these new regulations that every toy that goes on the market needs $40,000 of testing. And they establish that as law and then all the small toy makers say, 'Wait a minute; I make three toy trains a year – I can't do $40,000 of testing on this train.' So regulation for the most part usually favors the existing players, and they use regulation as an excuse to further entrench their own monopolies. That's of concern to me.

But I definitely believe in regulation done properly, with the right people at the table. It doesn't feel possible in today's government but yes, in principle. The main thing that I'm pushing for is, if regulation is like the way an allopathic doctor deals with disease by finding the drugs to kill that disease, I'm going more on the homeopathic side, saying, 'Okay, there's this disease there and let the regular medical doctors deal with that, but I'm going to strengthen your immune system.' That's what I'm trying to do with my work – strengthen our collective cultural immune system, so we're more resistant against this stuff.

Andrew Keen: Do you think the iPhone should come with a health warning, something like cigarette packets: 'This device might harm democracy or your humanity?'

Douglas Rushkoff: Would people stop using it?

Andrew Keen: Well, people are stopping smoking, eventually.

Douglas Rushkoff: They stop smoking but I don't know if it was because of the labels. It's interesting. Now they're starting again, of course – the problem in my daughter's middle school is they're all smoking Juuls. So the corporations come back around and re-addict us. I'm not any total fan of Steve Jobs, but I don't think the iPhone in its original form was going to be addictive. I don't think he meant for this to happen.

Andrew Keen: He didn't let his kids have an iPhone or an iPad in the house, so he knew something was wrong.

Douglas Rushkoff: Yes, that's the funny thing. Again, that was another motivation to write this book – I have evidence; I've spoken with the tech billionaires who are trying to earn enough money to insulate themselves from the reality they're creating.

They know they're destroying the world. They're building bunkers in New Zealand and Alaska, and they're trying to get away from us. They hate the world that they've made, but they feel trapped. So they're also the people I'm trying to help. You don't have to do it this way; maybe a business plan where you earn $10 or $50 million is enough, rather than $1 billion.

Andrew Keen: Finally Douglas, you're one of the great dreamers in tech and in cultural criticism. Let's forget practicalities – dream a little bit for me. Say we wake up in ten years. What does it look like very briefly, and what do we need to do to make this dream a reality?

Douglas Rushkoff: Well, those are two different questions. The world that we wake up in is one where people are sourcing their food from within 50 to 100 miles of where they live. They have a local currency that they use alongside the centrally issued US dollar. Their kids walk to a public school that they feel is safe enough for their kid to walk there. There's a lot fewer automobiles on the road because we've realized that light rail and other things are more efficient, and more people are working closer to their homes than they did before.

And we've established commonses for many of the things that we currently have markets for. I would say technologically the biggest change would be that our data is part of a commons. That there is no more marketing of our data, so Google and Facebook and Twitter and all these companies that are living off our data won't be able to do that anymore because we have a data commons, where we contribute all of the data that we want to that commons so that it could be used by anyone to do medical research or even consumer research or anything you want, so that data has no value because it's everybody's. It's no longer proprietary.

We adopt the principles of regenerative agriculture in economics and education and politics. We recall what it is to live with many more circles than lines, so we have a society that is no longer hell-bent on progress by any means necessary, a linear progress, and is looking instead at quality of life. And I don't think that's so outrageous – it's just a much more locally scaled existence, where the first alternative is to look for a friend to help you with something rather than to look for a product to accomplish it for you.

Andrew Keen: I feel we should end with a rendition of John Lennon's 'Imagine'.

Douglas Rushkoff: Yeah, except we don't just have to imagine it. I would say that if we are not actively moving toward that, we're all going to die. We no longer have the luxury of not engaging with these ancient indigenous practices. We're realizing, even as privileged white males, that we finally know what it is like to be colonized by the corporation, the same way the Native Americans knew what it was like to be colonized by the British East India Company or that Africa and South America knew what it was like to be colonized by America and Spain. Now we know what it is like to be colonized by apps that are colonizing our awareness, our data, our money, and our consciousness.

We can push back in some of the ways that you're talking about. They're not the ways I know about, but through democratic process, regulation, government, and activism. And we can push back by restoring our basic human decency, our ability to connect with other people. The more social you are, the more connected you are with other people, the more you can look in other people's eyes and not look away, the more resilience you will have, the more resistance you will be able to mount against a multi-trillion-dollar industry that means you no good.

ELI PARISER

Once upon a time, we believed that the internet enabled people of different opinions and cultures to talk to one another, but that was before Eli Pariser wrote his iconic book *The Filter Bubble: How the New Personalized Internet Is Changing What We Read and How We Think* in 2011. Pariser portrayed the internet as a mirror which reflected our own opinions and cultures in what we saw and read on it. Rather than stimulating conversation, Pariser proposed the internet was causing us to talk to ourselves.

For all his criticism of the digital revolution, Eli – like other digital pioneers such as David Kirkpatrick, Peter Sunde and Doug Rushkoff – remains a 'tomorrow'. As he tells me in our conversation, technology can still make the world a better place. However, it's interesting that his new faith is not in a new technology like blockchain or AI; instead, he's gone back to the city as a platform to enable people of different opinions to talk to one another. Digital technology still has value, Eli insists, but it won't fix the future. Only people can do that.

Andrew Keen: Eli Pariser, in our introductory chat I asked what's your one-liner and you said, 'Digital activist'. So what does that involve?

Eli Pariser: I like it because it's totally vague and opaque. I got my start thinking about the internet and democracy at MoveOn, and there the question was, how do you take these new tools provided by the internet and use them to make ordinary citizens more powerful with more of a voice in the political process?

And so that was kind of where I cut my teeth on these issues, but at MoveOn it became clear really quickly that the people who controlled the communications media that we used had a huge amount of power over the political process as well.

Andrew Keen: You joined MoveOn.org in 2004, which seems like a century ago in internet time.

Eli Pariser: Actually 2001 was when I started working with the founders.

Andrew Keen: How hopeful were you back then, 18 years ago, that the internet was going to be a platform that enabled radical political reform, particularly on the left given your politics?

Eli Pariser: I was very hopeful. And actually, even more than my particular political leanings, I was hopeful about the idea, which a lot of people were excited about then, that technology was inevitably going to decentralize power. And I think in a way, the arc of the last 18 years has been this increasing realization that not only is it not decentralizing power in a lot of ways, it's increasingly concentrating it. That's not a function of the technology per se – the technology could be used to decentralize or concentrate – but it turns out that existing incumbents and power structures are much harder to displace than people believed back in 2001.

Andrew Keen: Did you have a moment, a rude awakening, when you recognized that this beautiful dream you had of the internet wasn't going to be realized?

Eli Pariser: Well I do remember seeing an article at the time pointing out that blogs were a proxy for this idea of the decentralization of power and of audience. And someone noticed in 2007 that there were no new progressive blogs, that it had stopped, which seemed weird because the whole idea was that anyone could have a voice.

And in fact, the structure of the web linking system was yielding more consolidation of traffic toward big aggregators like *The Huffington Post* or the *New York Times* than distribution of traffic. And that was the first time that I started to wonder, is this whole thing going to turn out the way that we all expected, or are there other dynamics at play?

And I think what we've seen over the last ten years is that there are just extraordinary benefits to being the *New York Times* if you're in the media or being Facebook if you're in the attention business. And that those returns to scale are very strong.

Andrew Keen: So it's a winner-take-all economy, which given the network effect lends itself to the pre-existing big players and it's an increasingly hard market to break into – is that what you're saying?

Eli Pariser: Correct, and part of that is the nature of network effects, but part of it is also the way that these companies have thrown their weight around to block new competitors. So Facebook for a long time had a whole team whose only job was to find evidence of other apps that were gaining traction and figure out how to definitively block them from using Facebook to reach an audience, and then how to copy the features those apps were finding traction with. They were very successful with that and they still are.

And so again, it's a place where we're seeing the idea that this was some kind of even playing field – maybe it was in 1996, but it no longer is.

Andrew Keen: Before we get onto fixing those imbalances, let's talk about your book, *The Filter Bubble*, which I think more than any other book published in the early part of the twenty-first century exposed the way in which the web wasn't a place for debate, for civil interaction, but actually was a place where the tribes congregated in their own ideological corners.

Eli Pariser: Well, I had just stepped back from MoveOn and I'd been thinking about this question of the concentration of traffic and I started to kind of do some research to figure out what it meant that, increasingly, instead of spending time on news home pages, people were consuming information through social feeds like Facebook.

And I had actually just done this experiment where to get out of my own little liberal enclave I had made some friends who are more libertarian and conservative and added them as Facebook friends. And what I noticed was that they weren't showing up on Facebook and Facebook had essentially edited them out. And it wasn't doing that to censor them but it was doing it because it noticed that I wasn't clicking on their links as much as I was for my liberal friends.

And so the algorithm was happily optimizing to what it thought I was interested in. And I thought, if this is happening times a whole society, what does that mean for the ability to have a real conversation? And that's really what led me to write the book.

Andrew Keen: What do you think the role of government should be, particularly the US government, in terms of fighting misinformation online, whether it's propaganda from abroad or from other Americans?

Eli Pariser: If I can make an extended metaphor here, my sense is that the American information system is sick but that there are two things going on. Imagine someone who has an immune disorder which means that a common cold is much more likely to kill them. I think of the American information environment as the immune disorder that has been set in motion decades ago, which is the decline of a whole bunch of kind of civic capacities including the fairness doctrine, public media, civil associations, newspapers, and even just car culture and TV, which displaces a lot of the time that people had for civic life.

So you have this kind of increasingly frayed and atomized American community with media resources that were already kind of stretching and thinning, and then you introduced the internet and the social platforms, which turned out to be really great vectors for viral disease. So on the one hand you have to do something about the disease, because if you have a compromised immune system the common cold can kill you. But on the other hand, if you're not strengthening the immune system, in the long run you know you're toast.

Andrew Keen: So we're dealing with two parallel medical conditions, but to extend your metaphor, are you suggesting that the American government is a doctor and needs to address both of those?

Eli Pariser: Where that leads me is that because of the speech concerns, I'm much more comfortable with the government taking a strong role on the 'immune system piece' than I am with them taking a strong role on the moderation of speech online. And I think it's much more important that we know that people who are well informed are just less susceptible to a lot of the conspiracy theories and the false information that's out there.

So the question is, how do you build a strong fact-based information delivery system? And I think what most industrialized countries have found is that there is a funding component to that which at least partly involves the state. And that might be state news like exists in lots of parts of Europe, or it might be funding that allocates money toward civic news infrastructure. And as local newspapers and even local TV, which is still a big source of news, is just waning across America, I think we have to consider using some of the enormous profits that these tech companies are making that used to be driving that ecosystem, taxing some of it and reallocating it toward media that serves the public good.

Andrew Keen: Do you think that these platforms like Facebook and Google should be required by government to be more transparent about the way in which their algorithms work, so everyone can understand the filter bubble architecture of the web? You figured that out, but you were an insider – most people are totally mystified by the way this thing works.

Eli Pariser: I definitely think transparency is an important piece of the equation, but I don't think it's sufficient and that's where I think a lot of the kind of data rights piece is more powerful. It seems pretty clear to me that if you or I put information into an information service like Google or Facebook, we should be able to see it, change it, and delete it, and move it somewhere else. And it's one of the ironies of this moment that people talk a great game about disruption and competition but Facebook and Google are very anti-competitive, and creating a more competitive environment would be a big step forward in my view.

Freeing the data that we put in in the first place, and giving people more of a sense of ownership and control over that, to me is a much more powerful move because it allows for the possibility of someone coming along and challenging Facebook or Google.

Andrew Keen: Are you suggesting that the Europeans are doing it right with initiatives like GDPR?

Eli Pariser: Well, GDPR in its implementation was a mess and probably strengthened Facebook and Google, frankly. But I think that there are better designed versions of some of those concepts – the problem with GDPR was that it essentially tilted the playing field in favor of services that people were so deeply enmeshed in that they would give them approval for almost anything. And I think what you really want is something that allows a start-up that is providing some new service to draw on the skill and power of the existing incumbents.

And so if I could bring, for example, my entire lifetime search and email history to a new search entrant, that would give them a much better leg up to serve me well than if they have to spend ten or fifteen years recreating Google's growth curve. So to me, that would be one piece that I think is fairly uncontroversial. If you're talking to normal people, they ought to have that right and it could really change the market.

Andrew Keen: Eli, we started this conversation with you saying that your rude awakening about the web was recognizing the winner-take-all nature of the economy and the fact that for start-ups it wasn't a level playing field. What's your thinking on anti-trust and what the Europeans are doing, and what the Americans are trying to do to break the stranglehold of these trillion-dollar leviathans like Google, Amazon, and Facebook?

Eli Pariser: Well, I think it is a really important piece of the equation on a really important tool, but the challenge with anti-trust is that it takes years and years.

Andrew Keen: But you've got to start somewhere?

Eli Pariser: I'm not saying we shouldn't do it; I'm just saying there are limits. I think sometimes people imagine that alone will change everything, but I think beyond the literal consequences of what happens in court, there's also the fact that it checks the power of what are fairly unchecked entities, and to me that's almost more important. That when someone at one of these companies is thinking about doing something unethical or anti-competitive, to me it's really important that either some question marks emerge or a lawyer somewhere says, 'Hey, let's not do that.'

But I do think we actually need more of a paradigm shift than anti-trust alone will allow, in the sense that I don't think a world in which there are four digital giants instead of two is so much better. And I think part of that gets back to the immune system question, which I think we can get much clearer on what it is that we need and expect from these platforms and encourage or obligate them to build toward that.

Andrew Keen: You began at MoveOn.org 18 years ago, but what should digital activists now be focused on? Obviously, they need to earn an income, but what are the key issues that concern you? Is it monopolies of these huge companies? Is it privacy? Is it misinformation? If there's one thing, what do you think digital activism should be focused on right now?

Eli Pariser: It's hard, because there's so much important work that's happening, but I do think if there has to be one thing it is just a totally unprecedented fact of human existence that one individual would control so much of how 2.5 billion people communicate, and I'm talking about Zuckerberg. No matter how good he is, morally or ethnically, no matter how benign, I think we've learned from history that empires that have god-kings are not very durable institutions. And part of that is because one person with his particular life experience can't possibly imagine, empathize with, or respond to the billions of different life experiences that are using the platform. And he happens to be a wealthy white man from the West, and that point of view really doesn't accommodate the way that a lot of people are living and using the platforms.

So I think that if there isn't some kind of feedback loop that is enforced with power, history would say that this is a fragile system and bad things are going to happen. And I think they are.

I think if there are two issues, the second is the way that concentration of power interacts with societal inequities, which could be by race or by class or by the way that it shifts economic dynamics. To me the heart of what's challenging right now is the confluence of those two things.

Andrew Keen: Let's end on a more cheerful note than Mark Zuckerberg's power. I know you think there's one possible fix to a lot of this stuff, and that's cities. So very briefly, tell me why you're so hopeful that cities and the urban model could be a solution to many of our contemporary ills, digital and otherwise.

Eli Pariser: I do think cities offer a lot of hope. I've been working on a project called Civic Signals and part of the question that we've been trying to answer is what would we like platforms to *do* for us, not just to stop doing?

And as part of that, we started asking, if we think about platforms as spaces for social interaction, are there models for how to structure spaces well? And cities I think are some of our best models and they do offer hope. At times when you look at this whole thing, and think it's impossible for millions or billions of people who don't know each other to relate reasonably, well cities are the proof that it is possible. You can get a lot of people who are really different from each other together in ways where they don't just not kill each other, but actually create beautiful things and create value together.

I've been doing a deep dive on how we can take some of what has been learned in urban planning and urban design and apply it to the design of the virtual spaces where we're now spending a lot of time. And cities have had to deal with a bunch of these problems for centuries, so there are a lot of ideas that come from urban life that we could rely on.

But I also think it does come back to Zuckerberg in a way, in that cities are a mix of private and public institutions and the public spaces, the parks, the libraries, the town halls are really important as well. And so I think cities show it's possible but also that there's some missing pieces of our digital infrastructure that we really need to get building, and quickly.

I am optimistic that we can and I think, just like people gave up on cities, people are giving up on the internet. It's too soon to count it out; we just need to build a better one, and that's what I'm hoping to focus on going forward.

KENNETH CUKIER

'Big data' is a term often used to describe the digital revolution, particularly in its merger of AI and the internet of things. One of the world's leading authorities in this field is Kenn Cukier, *The Economist* senior editor and co-author of the 2013 bestseller *Big Data: A Revolution That Will Transform How We Live, Work and Think.* But not all is well in the land of big data, as Cukier explained when we met at *The Economist* offices in central London in 2019.

In our conversation, Kenn acknowledges that he began as a believer in the benefits of big data, taking for granted that it would improve how we live, work, and think. However, the problem, as he explains, is that this big data revolution has been transformed by Silicon Valley leviathans such as Google and Facebook into what Shoshana Zuboff calls 'surveillance capitalism'. And so, he warns, big data is destroying not only our individual privacy but also our democracy. Despite this, like Kirkpatrick, Sunde, Pariser, and Rushkoff, Cukier remains a 'tomorrow', but insists that we need business models that respect, rather than destroy, our individual privacy.

Andrew Keen: Kenn Cukier, senior editor at *The Economist* and co-author of the bestselling, iconic *Big Data*, is democracy in trouble?

Kenn Cukier: Democracy is in big trouble. It's in trouble in many different dimensions. In terms of technology, many people would say it's in trouble because of platforms like Facebook and Google that can be manipulated. And that's true, but it's in trouble for so many other reasons as well and we really need to disentangle all the various ways, because the solutions are going to be different.

And one way it's going to be in trouble is because of the manipulation that can happen for electoral campaigns over big web platforms. The risk in democracies is the degree to which data about people is going to be centralized by the state and whether protections for people will be guaranteed.

Andrew Keen: You're an expert in technology, bestselling author of *Big Data*. Is it coincidental that this crisis of democracy has happened at the same time as the digital revolution?

Kenn Cukier: They're joined at the hip, in parallel, and the reason why is that the internet and the web and social media is fundamentally different from the traditional media, and it allows for community formation across time and space in a way that was never possible before. And so fringe interests that could never self-identify and rally together and be cohesive now finally could.

And so what was the discrete opinion of a supremacist in North Carolina and another supremacist in Denver can now join forces and they can bring other people onto their side. And so where before we had this homogenization of public opinion through three broadcast networks and maybe five national dailies and so things devolved down to a milquetoast mean of mainstream opinion, now that you have the atomization of the public sphere you have lots of different interests that can find each other and find common cause.

And so how else would you organize a Unite the Right march in Charlottesville and have a lot of neo-Nazis in America come together and feel a legitimization of their views because of safety in numbers?

Andrew Keen: I accept that argument, but isn't there a counterargument that without the internet you wouldn't have had the democratic initiatives of MeToo, of Black Lives Matter, of the Occupy movement?

Kenn Cukier: Of course. The Lord giveth, the Lord taketh away. And Zuck giveth, Zuck taketh away as well, so it's both good and bad. I personally believe that it's infinitely better than it is bad, although this remains to be seen because experience is not going in my direction.

Andrew Keen: But you're the one who's talking about the demise or crisis of democracy.

Kenn Cukier: True, but I'm not talking about the demise of civilization. Our democratic institutions are strained.

Andrew Keen: Well, in a sense civilization and democracy are the same thing, aren't they?

Kenn Cukier: It depends on how you define it. Look, I'm very worried about the moment that we're in. I don't think it's entirely the internet's fault, but the internet is going to be part of the solution as well as part of the problem.

However, what I do know is that the internet certainly fueled and was an amplifier to the populists and the people whom they pandered to, who got so energized that it brought them into office, and who have the fringe of views and whose values are not the ones that in the past the mainstream accepted.

So the mainstream has to make the case with more muscularity about why some of these boring things like checks and balances actually matter, because we're on the back foot – we being the classical nineteenth-century liberals of the modern era who believe in things like rule of law and process and fairness and a state that protects rights. We need to make the case with a verve that we've never done before that we need these boring things that make a fair and a just society. We took them for granted and we can't anymore because they're being eroded.

Andrew Keen: How is immigration playing into the crisis of democracy? Can one be a nationalist and a populist and a democrat?

Kenn Cukier: Yeah. Being a nationalist isn't a particular problem – I think the nation is a very good entity to rally people around together and you can have a very good, wholesome nationalism. I think a lot of Americans of our generation felt that wholesome nationalism. I think Americans of a certain age, I put the age around 50, will remember the first time they traveled through Europe or in Asia and came across other Americans. This is 25 years ago and they'd say, 'Hey, where are you from?' And the person would say, 'I'm from Arizona. Where are you from?' 'I'm from New Jersey.' This is the same distance as St Petersburg and Paris, and in some ways these people would be as disparate as someone from Russia and a Parisian – totally different but at the same time there was this commonality, there was a *civitas*. There was this common glue among them that they felt of one nation. What was the cause of that? Was it conscription in Korea, Vietnam, and World War II? Was it about the flag, was it about mainstream television from *The Muppet Show* and Peter Jennings, the television broadcaster, in the evening? In fact, it was all of that.

That has completely changed now. The Red State and the Blue State has become this yawning gap as has never existed before. You can have a responsible nationalism, and we don't have that right now. But populism is different – the whole nature of populism is that it is a four-letter word.

Andrew Keen: To us, but not to everybody.

Kenn Cukier: Well, to a political scientist, if you're calling something populist, you're saying—

Andrew Keen: Because they're irrational?

Kenn Cukier: No, because it's mob rule, it's really just about pandering to the people for a self-interested governance and not a governance that would be truly democratic, which is to say a state that not only that looks to the best for people and that drives its power based on the people of self-governance because the majority has elected it, but has protections and rights for people with minority views.

Who used free speech? Free speech was used by the Civil Rights Movement. Free speech was used by women who were arguing for contraception in places where the mere talk of it was seen as advocating murder and you could put them into jail.

Eugene V. Debs, the great socialist who got 6 per cent of the vote in 1912, was condemned for free speech. And why was his conviction upheld? His free speech was opposing the draft during World War I. The whole point about free speech is that it's used by minority interests and for minority views.

Steve Bannon and others use it today. Is it a misuse of free speech protections for this heinous outlook on the world? Sadly, no – the whole point about free speech and the whole point about a state that protects rights is to protect rights that you find noxious and heinous. Hopefully in the past it was that more speech would crowd out the bad speech. I think that might be a naive approach of thinking about it, a very seventeenth- or eighteenth-century view of free speech. In a world in which we have this huge abundance of speech because of the internet, maybe we need other institutions and practices to protect truth in the fog of mistruth and bad speech.

We're in new territory, but the whole point about the state and democracy is that it guarantees rights to people, and the nature of the populist is that they're actually pandering.

To answer your question, we need a nationalism that is responsible. We need a civic glue that we're losing in a world of social media where the public sphere is atomized, but we don't need populists.

Andrew Keen: How excited are you by the impact of big data on democracy? Is this the solution? Is this the way out of our dilemma?

Kenn Cukier: No. I'm really excited about the potential for big data, for AI, in all domains of society and I think it *could* be used responsibly in politics. But so far, we're mostly seeing it being misused. How could it be used responsibly? You might if you wanted to get a sense of what public opinion is on something or how to make a government website work better – you could collect the data. These are really pedestrian examples, I realize…

Andrew Keen: Is anyone doing that? The Estonians or the Dutch?

Kenn Cukier: Even in America – it turns out that under the Obama Administration they had a digital service that was looking at where people were giving up or clicking out of a government website, so they could know what features to build into it to improve the functionality of that website. It was kind of basic; they were just applying a Silicon Valley approach to product management to create things for politics. And that's viable and good, but more interesting are the pathologies that we're seeing because it's being misused more than it's being used.

Andrew Keen: Where is it being misused?

Kenn Cukier: Cambridge Analytica and Facebook is the biggest example of that.

Andrew Keen: Explain how Cambridge Analytica and Facebook have been undermining democracy.

Kenn Cukier: We've always presumed that by putting the political candidate in democracy in the public sphere that we could all examine that person's views and come to a community-based agreement on whether this person would lead or not.

But we never had a politics in which a candidate could whisper in everyone's ear completely independently and no one else could hear it. But the way that micro-targeting works on a platform like Facebook, with the data from someone like Cambridge Analytica, is they're able to take the hot-button issues at the individual level of a cohort of, say, the whole population of the United States, and then micro-target to their particular interest, whether it's being a gun lover or racism or sexism, and we can press your buttons either to create apathy around you so you don't go out to the polls or to spur you up and arouse you so you do go out to the polls.

Cambridge Analytica, in the Trump campaign, did not take Americans and turn them into racists; they took racists and turned them into voters. And that is the problem that we have: when you have a fragmented public sphere and you're able to have these micro-conversations, these tiny whispers to people. They're not even aware they're being manipulated – they didn't know if they were being manipulated by Russia. Whether it's being done by Russia, by another campaign, or whether it's being done by a political action committee that's funded by a big financier; we don't know these things.

And so we lose the transparency that democracy has always relied on, because of the technology and because of the lack of rules around that technology. We need to improve the rules, knowing that the technology has this potential for a pathology baked into it.

Andrew Keen: Cambridge Analytica and Facebook are private companies, but governments are also abusing big data in terms of undermining or even destroying democracy. Can you talk about that, and particularly the Chinese model?

Kenn Cukier: I would challenge it a little bit because most democracies so far are not really using big data to undermine democracy. In fact, a lot of countries are using it to actually improve it. For example, there's lots of 'nudge units', which change the default settings such as saving for a pension, and say that if you have public institutions wisely using data about citizens you can get to better outcomes.

Andrew Keen: So it's great for behavioral economists, at least at the state level?

Kenn Cukier: If they have responsible outcomes like getting people to recycle or save energy or use a seatbelt or not drink and drive, that's great. So where is it a trouble? We're already seeing the canary in the coalmine is suffocated and dead in China when it comes to big data, artificial intelligence, and state surveillance. For the Uyghurs in particular, but elsewhere throughout China for facial recognition.

That to me is troubling and to be honest is making me really reconsider my views and my optimism about big data, because as I see what's going on in terms of how data is being used in China for repression and what's happening in the West in the rise of populism, authoritarianism, and the rise of artificial intelligence, I realize that I've seen this movie before.

Andrew Keen: Is this the twenty-first-century version of Orwell's *1984*?

Kenn Cukier: I hate historical analogies, because if that was only the case it looks tame. I'm really not an alarmist, but the whole point of *1984* was that Winston Smith could circumvent the surveillance that he had – there was a place in his building in which he could avoid the telescreen. I don't think we can avoid the telescreen anymore and that's why I'm nervous. And the Snowden disclosures have given me a lot of alarm that even in democracies we have well-meaning public officials in the intelligence community, whose job is to keep us safe, who are bending the rules in a way that I think that we should as citizens in America be uncomfortable with. Because if we're going to grant the state these powers to collect and analyze data, we want to make sure it's done under the rule of law.

The system that's been set up in the US is actually a very good system. But the process by which the safeguards were upheld was not obeyed, and so that was the problem.

Andrew Keen: What's the best way to counter the Chinese model?

Kenn Cukier: It's such a good question. I think for a Chinese person it's going to have to be individual disinformation, in which you try your best to circumvent it left, right, and center, and I think honestly it might be a very failing mechanism. I wouldn't want to rely on it and I've only begun to think seriously about this. I don't have a very good answer but I'm very troubled by it.

In the West it's really about getting the institutions right, getting the rule of law right, and having not just the regulations but the enforcement of it with teeth. If there were mass firings after the Snowden disclosures, I would feel more relieved. If Equifax, after their hack, was liquidated and its assets stripped and sold, I would feel like there was true muscular regulation around privacy, both from the business side and the government side. But we didn't have that.

In fact, the reforms under Obama were cosmetic and everyone involved kept their job, even those who lied to senators in Congressional testimony, notably James Clapper who lied to Senator Wyden about whether he collected information on Americans.

—

PETER SUNDE

There's one conversation with Peter Sunde, co-founder of the music-sharing network The Pirate Bay, that I'll always remember. It took place in around 2012 in Belgrade Airport, as we were returning from a tech conference in Serbia. Peter and I strongly disagreed about the value of online intellectual property, yet we were on good terms personally. So I was shocked when he told me, as we sat in the airport lounge, that he was being sent to jail for his role at The Pirate Bay.

Peter did indeed go to jail for several months in 2014, but since his release he has become more of an intellectual friend than an enemy. He has radically shifted his opinion of the digital revolution, going from a file-sharing utopian to a sceptic of the monopolistic and often exploitative nature of the digital economy. And yet, as you can tell from this conversation from June 2019, he remains a 'tomorrow' and believes that smart technology, if deployed intelligently, can still make the world a better place.

Andrew Keen: Peter Sunde, the co-founder of The Pirate Bay, you can't quite remember when you founded The Pirate Bay or when it founded you, but you think it was around 2002 or 2003. What were you trying to do? Were you trying to democratize the web and the world?

Peter Sunde: No. We don't really remember when it was founded or who was part of it; the only thing we remember was that it was a fun project, and that there were no grand plans about it.

Andrew Keen: But what was it? What's your claim to fame? Why has it made you into a digital celebrity up there with Julian Assange and Edward Snowden?

Peter Sunde: I think Pirate Bay became a community for people that didn't want the internet to become a place just for markets. In the core group of Pirate Bay, we were three different people with three different political beliefs, but I think what united us was that we wanted an internet that was controlled by the people and not by companies. And I think that struck a chord with people even back then, when we saw that companies started to take over the internet and were controlling it more and more.

Andrew Keen: So what does that mean, 'controlled by the people'? Does that mean that people own the content on the internet and does it mean that they were empowered? What were you trying to do – empower people and disrupt all the industries?

Peter Sunde: I think it was about not accepting that companies regulated the internet. We did a lot of promotions for people to vote in elections; we didn't tell people what to vote but we wanted people to engage more, and I think that's the core of it – we wanted people to discuss the issues of intellectual property, freedom of speech, and the access to information.

That was why essentially Pirate Bay became much bigger than the other platforms that did the same: it was not just about the piracy but it was also about why we had piracy and why we wanted it.

Andrew Keen: When you look back at it now, I know you're ambivalent in some ways about the experience of Pirate Bay and its achievements, but what do you think was its greatest accomplishment?

Peter Sunde: I would say that it made people think a little bit more and not just swallow propaganda from the corporate industry.

Andrew Keen: So it's a kind of democratizer, or at least an information democratizer?

Peter Sunde: Definitely; it's an eye-opener. And I think it's also kind of like the David and Goliath story.

Andrew Keen: So Peter, you were a young technologist who had a vision, an idea, a dream of democratizing culture, of using technology to do it and in a sense you succeeded. Pirate Bay became one of the best known platforms for the exchange of content, and yet it didn't quite work out in the way you expected, did it?

Peter Sunde: Yes and no. I travel way too much and I go to some countries that don't have a market and people will come up to me and explain in perfect English how important Pirate Bay has been for getting access to, let's say Photoshop, so that they can get into graphics and now they have a high-paying job because of that, or they learned to speak English so they could get a job as a support engineer somewhere. And people are always coming up to me when I travel to explain this. And this is always in countries where these big companies are not interested in having a market. So for me that's a really big success.

Andrew Keen: So in a sense, it's still democratized culture, in a way that gave underprivileged people in smaller markets the opportunity to access the dominant culture, the language, the entertainment?

Peter Sunde: In one way yes, but in the other way I don't like what Pirate Bay has become. When we started it we made a decision that when Pirate Bay turned ten years old we would close it down – we didn't want it to become like a behemoth, like a monopoly.

Andrew Keen: So let's personalize this a little bit, Peter. You may not be Julian Assange or Edward Snowden, but your narrative is an interesting one. What happened to you that's such a striking and I assume a rather disturbing narrative? You went to jail, right? You became this public enemy number one in Sweden and the epitome of an internet pirate, and you got the book thrown at you by the law. Is that fair?

Peter Sunde: Yes, I went to jail, but I got a few hundred letters per day.

Andrew Keen: How long did you go to jail for?

Peter Sunde: I ended up spending six months in jail, for aiding with possible copyright infringements.

Andrew Keen: So basically enabling stealing online?

Peter Sunde: It's not stealing Andrew – you know this. It's very different from stealing because stealing deprives someone.

Andrew Keen: Well, it's taking somebody else's property.

Peter Sunde: And it was aiding with aiding.

Andrew Keen: So aiding the aiders? So you're not actually aiding?

Peter Sunde: No; we're aiding the aiders, which is, let's call it 'the stretch'.

Andrew Keen: So you went to jail and I think the interesting twist in the narrative here is that I wouldn't say that you've had your own 'digital road to Damascus moment', but you've certainly changed your opinion about the internet and even about Pirate Bay. When did you come out of jail?

Peter Sunde: Four years ago, I think.

Andrew Keen: And over the last few years, you've changed – is that fair?

Peter Sunde: No, I think the internet changed. And I think that's why we've been on opposite sides of this before.

Andrew Keen: You mean you and me?

Peter Sunde: Yeah. I had this idea of what the internet could become and we were on a path...

Andrew Keen: You mean this ideal of democratization?

Peter Sunde: Yes, and the potential of the internet making things better. And then it slowly became the opposite.

Andrew Keen: Was there a moment, when you saw what Facebook was doing, when you saw how powerful Google was, when you realized, 'Oh my God, this is really going wrong'?

Peter Sunde: I have a friend who's a music video producer, and he uploaded his music videos to Facebook. They took them down because he didn't have the copyright for the music in the videos, and he explained to Facebook that he made these videos.

Andrew Keen: So they were his own work?

Peter Sunde: His work. And they said they included copyrighted music and he said, 'But this is my portfolio.' So he uploaded them again and Facebook turned off his possibility of uploading videos and said, 'We told you not to have these on Facebook.' They were not upset that he uploaded them or because of the potential copyright infringement but because he didn't do what they told him.

So then he changed his profile pictures to a huge cock and said, 'Fuck Facebook,' so they banned him from Facebook. And what happened was that for a while he no longer had a normal social life because everyone had started inviting people to birthday parties and updating people about everything going on in their life on Facebook. So he could literally sit on a Saturday evening not at a party because people didn't invite him, because he was not on Facebook, and his friends didn't know. He just vanished. And they didn't only delete his account; they deleted pictures that he was tagged in from other people's accounts.

Andrew Keen: So that woke you up; that made you realize that this thing has gone profoundly wrong?

Peter Sunde: They erased him from outside the internet as well, not only from Facebook but it also affected his life outside of the internet dramatically, to the level that his friends no longer talked to him the same way because they just assumed that if you invite everyone to an event on Facebook everyone will come.

Andrew Keen: So what was most troubling to you about that anecdote? Was it the new authoritarianism of companies like Facebook? Was it the fact that they could ruin people's lives willfully, without even any thought? Because presumably on the Facebook side it was some small-time bureaucrat somewhere making these decisions – it wasn't exactly Mark Zuckerberg, right?

Peter Sunde: Or maybe it was because of Mark Zuckerberg that they made that kind of decision.

Andrew Keen: Or even an algorithm, right; I mean, it may not have even been a person behind it.

Peter Sunde: For me, the thing that was troubling was that we somehow slid into this situation where this would happen and have such effects on everyday life and we never had a discussion about the rules and regulations. And every time you talked about regulating the internet it was not about how to regulate the big corporations and how to get users' rights. In Finland we made the internet a human right; the only country in the world that I know that did this.

Andrew Keen: So that's the Scandinavian solution: making the internet a human right?

Peter Sunde: Yeah, but I think that the focus has always been on regulating what you *cannot* do on the internet and what you *cannot* do in society because basically the internet and society are the same thing, it is just a different medium for the same discussions. So for me, that was the troubling situation where we didn't have the rights as users anymore; we didn't have the normal rights and we didn't talk about them. The discourse was always on how to ban things the users were doing instead of making sure that we had the rights to freedom of speech, ownership of our own data, controlling our own identity.

Andrew Keen: One of the guys we've had on this show, John Borthwick, the CEO of Betaworks, is a well-known investor in New York and he thinks that there isn't that much difference between Facebook and China. Are you suggesting the same thing – that they're both intrinsically authoritarian?

Peter Sunde: Of course they are. The problem is that we willingly select to be on Facebook, whereas to be in China you either have to move there or you have to be born there. I think Facebook is a little bit worse because in many ways you have this idea that Facebook is your friend; in China, much like in Stasi Germany, people knew who their enemy was. You were aware of being spied on. And when you talked to people, you knew how to behave. There's certain codes in both China and in Stasi Germany – you know whom you can't talk to and what you can't talk about. On Facebook you don't think about it; it just happens. And that is really problematic.

Andrew Keen: Are the Facebook guys worse than the copyright industry? Are they equivalent or are they different?

Peter Sunde: Facebook is a bit worse because they meddle so much more with democracy. But they operate in the same space because they just see money rather than social impact and social responsibilities. I think social responsibility for Zuckerberg is that he doesn't have to go to Congress or to the European Parliament and be held responsible for things. He doesn't want to have social responsibilities on Facebook.

Andrew Keen: So ten years ago, everyone talked about Facebook being behind the trigger of the Arab Spring, of democratizing movements all over the world. Today we seem to have a shift toward authoritarianism, whether it's Putin, Trump, Erdogan, Bolsonaro, or what's happening in Italy, Poland, Hungary. Do you see a connection between the corruption of the digital dream and the crisis of democracy around the world?

Peter Sunde: I think with the internet and globalization combined, we live in a world where everything is becoming the same in each country. And the problem is that for some reason you're going to take the worst of each country and use that instead of the best of each country. I think that the success of Trump bred the situation for Bolsonaro and other people to take control of different countries, and this all comes down to the internet being used the way it is. I wouldn't say the technology is responsible...

Andrew Keen: But the two things are connected and they're working together in parallel – it's like a ball of yarn where they're tied together; is that fair?

Peter Sunde: Definitely, and I think that people still have in their mind that the internet is a liberating medium that gives you some sort of freedom.

Andrew Keen: I can't believe that the co-founder of Pirate Bay, one of the platforms that enabled this, is actually saying that. That's a fairly radical shift in your thinking, isn't it?

Peter Sunde: I think it's the shift of the internet rather than my world. I went to a really interesting festival in Copenhagen called Techfestival and we had a sit-down with 150 people who are entrepreneurs or activists or people interested in social justice, people interested in technologies and how technologies can change the world. And people from big corporations, big media industries, and everyone agreed that the internet had got kind of out of hand. So I'm definitely not alone in this kind of view, but I think our own naivety is the reason for all of this because we didn't regulate, we didn't decide the rules.

Andrew Keen: It's quite striking that the co-founder of Pirate Bay would be saying that the solution is regulation.

Peter Sunde: I've always been in favor of regulation if it's for the usage of the personal individual using the internet.

Andrew Keen: This is such a complicated problem. What comes first, fixing the internet or fixing democracy? What should our priority be? Should we be more worried about this corruption of the internet or about the corruption of democracy, or are they so bound up with one another, that to fix one would inevitably mean fixing the other?

So more regulation, as the Europeans are doing? Anti-trust, regulation around data privacy, regulation on taxes, regulation on the accountability of these platforms; is that the kind of regulation you're discussing?

Peter Sunde: Either that, which is the sane way of doing it, or we have a revolution which I don't see happening but I would prefer it because it would be much quicker.

Andrew Keen: You would?

Peter Sunde: Yes. We should take the internet ownership back and redistribute the resources. Why does Denmark have more IP addresses than all of Africa? We mimicked all the shit in real-life society on the internet.

Andrew Keen: So taking the internet back is something that people like Tim Berners-Lee are now trying to do – it's not just a pipe dream. Some of the pioneers of the original architecture of the internet are dedicated to that and you're certainly an influential figure. Do you think more and more people are trying to do this?

Peter Sunde: But like you say, Tim Berners-Lee and other people are talking about taking the internet back, but when I was talking about these things before, I was viewed as a rebel for doing this, but I think people started to agree with the views I had about who would control the internet, who creates algorithms, like Google with their page rank; there's a democratic deficit if you don't have transparency into these questions. Why did Facebook decide to filter out this or that news thing? We need to regulate them so that we know what they're doing and we need transparency in these areas.

Andrew Keen: And could the technology of file-sharing networks like Pirate Bay be a solution to some of this, for example to filtering out fake news?

Peter Sunde: Yes and no. I think we shouldn't put too much hope into technologies fixing the problems of technologies. I think that's a pipe dream.

Andrew Keen: Even blockchain?

Peter Sunde: Blockchain is just the worst of it, because that's an ultra-libertarian dream.

Andrew Keen: Or Bitcoin?

Peter Sunde: I think that besides the CO_2 emissions from that industry, which is just insane, it's like a pyramid scheme – from the people who had Bitcoins in the beginning and the people hoping to become the next guys who have a lot of Bitcoins. It doesn't bring any value; the only thing that Bitcoin prices surging has done is that activists who want to use Bitcoin in other things can't really afford it because the prices fluctuate. The idea of using these distributed, decentralized cryptocurrencies, which was kind of the sales point at the beginning, because of the capitalism on top of that, had fucked up that industry. It's like fixing the system from within the system, with the system's regulations – it's really hard to do and I don't think a lot of people would think that that's a sane idea.

Andrew Keen: When are we going to get a book out of you on all this? On your life and on your views on capitalism, on the digital revolution, on Pirate Bay, on Facebook?

Peter Sunde: I've written 5,000 pages so far and it's way too much, so I have to cut it.

Andrew Keen: And you began that in prison?

Peter Sunde: No, way before; in prison I wrote a sitcom.

Andrew Keen: And did that ever get published?

Peter Sunde: No – after I'm done with the current TV series I'm doing, that's the next project.

Andrew Keen: And has all this writing changed your opinion of the copyright industry? When you have a bestseller, are you going to put it on Pirate Bay?

Peter Sunde: I hope someone else is going to put it on Pirate Bay so I can sue them, because I know everything about it. And that would be great PR.

PART 3

DEMOCRACY AND ITS DIGITAL DISCONTENT

—

PETER POMERANTSEV

What's so bad about believing in yesterday, some people might ask? After all, aren't 'yesterdays' just conservatives with a reverence for historic institutions and traditional ideas? But as the disinformation expert Peter Pomerantsev explained to me when we met in London in 2019, today's 'yesterdays' are exemplified by Vladimir Putin and his nostalgia for the twentieth-century Soviet Union. Putin's Russia is pioneering a particularly corrosive kind of 'yesterday-ism' – one that is now being imitated by Erdogan, Trump, Duterte, Orbán, and Bolsonaro.

Pomerantsev is particularly good at explaining how 'yesterdays' are using technology to wreck today's world, explaining that it has become the primary battleground for Putin's trolls, who flood the internet with lies. As for Pomerantsev's solutions to the disinformation war, he argues that rather than censoring the internet, we need to make Facebook or Google's algorithms more transparent, so that we can understand the architecture of the information economy.

Andrew Keen: Peter Pomerantsev, the author of *This Is Not Propaganda: Adventures in the War Against Reality*, you have fashioned yourself as the authority on the propaganda of Putin's Russia. Is that fair?

Peter Pomerantsev: The only authority I have is from having worked inside the Russian TV system, which I suppose gave me some insights as to the psychology of the system that produces it. And because I was working for Russian entertainment TV, not news, I had to spend a lot of my time thinking about Russian audiences and talking to Russian producers about how they think, about mass influence essentially. I guess that gave me a semi-insider's view, but the rest is just interpretation.

Andrew Keen: So you've made your name as a writer and as an analyst of Putin's Russia on the idea that Putin invented an alternative reality, a kind of reality television version of politics. Is that a fair way to describe your description of Putin's Russia?

Peter Pomerantsev: Without a doubt, there are two things: (a) the Soviets already had an obsession with propaganda, not merely as a formatter of public opinion but kind of as a creator of the new communist man. And the propagandist was already a sort of demigod in the Soviet system. And it's very important to understand this tradition that already existed. It's a very exalted role that they gave to propagandists. And with no shame attached to it; quite the opposite. And the first

146

thing that Putin does when he comes to power is grab control of television, even before he's grabbed control of the energy companies, the security system. So only he and the people around him realized that TV would be the essence of power. Almost an ersatz for power, because actually the state was still quite weak; the oligarchs were still very strong. There was not a crazy risk of the country falling apart, and really the way they bound the country and held it together was through the power of media.

Andrew Keen: How important is the spirit of nostalgia in the ideology of Putinism, this idea that the past was better?

Peter Pomerantsev: I think it's very interesting to look at the development of that and to see why Russia is the forerunner to America, Europe, Latin America…

Andrew Keen: Hungary, the Philippines, everywhere basically?

Peter Pomerantsev: My version of this is that essentially Russia got to the state that everybody else is at now a lot earlier.

Andrew Keen: So ironic that the Russians were first for once, wasn't it?

Peter Pomerantsev: Ironic because they lost – Russia was the country where all kinds of ideas about a better future and progress collapsed the earliest – obviously communism, which no one really believed in. The key thing is that in Russia, all the ideas of the future we had fell away first. And then, if there's no idea of the future anymore, all that's left are various forms of nostalgia. Already by the late 1990s Svetlana Boym, who is a great Harvard expert on the idea of nostalgia, is writing about Russia in ways you can write about the West now.

The 1990s started with all these utopias and they're just finishing with completely different types of nostalgia. That's the only mode of thinking left. Now the one thing you don't need in nostalgia is facts. That's not a mental architecture where facts are useful or necessary. And when you have a version of the future you need facts to prove that you're getting to this future.

Andrew Keen: So they're rather vulgar post-modernists – for them facts are meaningless?

Peter Pomerantsev: Yeah. Some of them even use some of the rhetoric of post-modernism, not that they've necessarily read it but they've just heard it. 'There are no facts, only interpretations – get off my back.' When you have politicians saying 'fuck facts', then…

Andrew Keen: Do they ever say that literally?

Peter Pomerantsev: No, but that's the attitude that there is and there's almost a teenage rebellion in that.

Andrew Keen: Is it surprising that Putin's favorite Beatles song is 'Yesterday'?

Peter Pomerantsev: I did not know he had a favorite Beatles song, but now that you've said it, it definitely works for the myth of Putin. And knowing Putin's spin doctors, maybe they put that out there on purpose to underscore his nostalgist credentials.

Andrew Keen: Well, before we get to how to fight nostalgia, your new book focuses on the way in which this post-Soviet zeitgeist has been exported to the West. When did you realize that the Russian experience was in some senses universal?

Peter Pomerantsev: I don't think it's been exported; I think the same processes are happening here, and the simple explanation would be that they started happening here after a series of political and economic disasters...

Andrew Keen: In 2008 and 2009?

Peter Pomerantsev: We can find lots of places.

Andrew Keen: Through globalization?

Peter Pomerantsev: Globalization is a bit vague for me, but what's certainly interesting is it could have happened in lots of places. So in Mexico it happened in a different way and kind of like that. They thought that after their own changes in 1989 they could have a better country, and it's not turned out very well.

So it's happened in different ways in different places, but a lot of countries have reached the same kind of conclusion as the Russians – that all versions of the future aren't getting us anywhere. Or rather, enough people in every country feel that.

Andrew Keen: So people have stopped believing in the future and started to reinvent the nostalgia of the past, to fetishize the past, whether it's Putin or Bolsonaro or Orbán or Duterte or Grillo. They're all really doing the same thing.

Peter Pomerantsev: And there could be something else going on there, something more systemic in the sense that the idea of the future for a long time was this competition between the Soviet system and the Western system. And they were kind of predicated on each other, even apart from the disasters of 2008 and other catastrophes. It's almost as if when the Soviet system disappeared, there was nothing left to compete with. We were kind of competing with ourselves which was always going to end up in a bad place.

Andrew Keen: How much of the populist crisis in the West, if that's the right word, can be explained by Russian meddling, Russian investment in trolls, Russian investment in neo-authoritarian, sometimes even neo-Nazi, groups who are fundamentally opposed to traditional democratic institutions?

Peter Pomerantsev: Well, it depends where you are. In the Ukraine it's been invaded so there it's like it's the war. We call it hybrid war but it's a war. And in some of the frontline states you have these massive Russian populations so there's a slightly different dynamic.

Andrew Keen: Certainly in the Baltics, right?

Peter Pomerantsev: Yeah, generally all responsibility comes from one's self, so I certainly wouldn't look for an outside cause. However, Russia is playing these margins with a kind of strategy and with a lot of tactics and there's something incredibly powerful in this sense that there's a beacon for these people. It's very hard to measure that effect. It's just the sense that there's a big guy out there who will help you, who has got your back, who will give you money; he doesn't give a toss about the global rules. That's very hard to quantify but if it wasn't there we'd definitely still have these issues, but it just gives it another level. That's so hard to quantify but I think that's the most important thing and the fact is that what Putin really caught was the trolly tone, that satirical, nasty, trolly tone that we see on the internet, that Salvini has and that all these guys have – Putin has had it for a long time.

Andrew Keen: A kind of aggressive nihilism.

Peter Pomerantsev: Aggressive nihilism with a lot of resentment.

Andrew Keen: Can we blame him? Could this have happened without the internet? If we still had traditional newspapers, if we didn't have Facebook and 4chan and YouTube and Instagram?

Peter Pomerantsev: To what extent is it technology-based? Firstly, I saw this happen inside Russia before the new technology hit, so it was already there. I think we saw it in America with the emergence of cable news, and so this was already happening, but without a doubt the internet and especially the algorithmic logic of social media – links and stuff like that, the way social media is geared around polarizing extreme emotions and rewards, and the ad tech system is based on that, almost like these politicians who are purposefully scandalous because they know that the ad tech system likes that discourse in order to get virility.

I think that has turbocharged it, without a doubt. Politicians do change according to the media. TV almost produces its own genre of politicians, and I think social media is also producing its own genre of politicians.

Andrew Keen: Who would be the quintessential? Trump, I assume?

Peter Pomerantsev: Salvini is really good, but Putin called the tone before a lot of these guys were really around.

Andrew Keen: How do we fight back? How do we fight back on behalf of the values that I'm guessing you and I share, the value of facts, of truth, of democracy, of the rights of minorities? How do we fight back against the world that you have so brilliantly described in your last two books?

Peter Pomerantsev: Well there's three problems, I think, and we often get them confused because they're interconnected, but it helps to disaggregate them if we're thinking of actionable things.

What is the Russia problem? It won't be solved in the information sphere, because the costs to Russia for its firehose of bullshit are virtually zero. No one is going to invade them because of a troll campaign. The costs are zero. They don't care if they're caught lying. And it's very cheap. We can slow them down, we can have fact-checking organizations, but we'll never win that.

However, the Russians have other vulnerabilities. It's a country in a dilemma where it needs confrontation with the West to secure national cohesion but it also needs a lot of economic relations with the West, down to selling oil and gas to us.

The place to hurt Russia would not be in the information space, so it's about political warfare and it's about having the political will to do it – it's the economic side where they're weak. So that's the Russia problem. There is no magical thing we can do with Putin, apart from sensible stuff like through journalism.

Secondly, there's an information problem, and there's a deep paradox here that we really haven't worked out how to deal with. Nineteen eighty-nine was meant to be the victory of free speech over censorship. There were metaphors that we all used: 'We live in a marketplace of ideas where the best products will win,' which is about freedom of expression. The more people speak the better democracy will be; the better debate will be. That's the old formula that fallacious information is countered with more and better information.

Andrew Keen: So truth wins out.

Peter Pomerantsev: It was kind of a market idea as well – the more you have, the best stuff wins. And that's turned out to be absolute nonsense, a bit like pure free market economics turned out to be absolute nonsense as well.

Andrew Keen: The reverse, in some senses is true.

Peter Pomerantsev: Clearly. I wouldn't undo freedom of expression, but yes. Censorship nowadays isn't done by constricting speech – it's about flooding the information space with so much bullshit that people don't know what the hell is going on anymore.

Even aggressive campaigns against opposition and dissidents are not done through secret police. They're done through troll farms, who just destroy someone's reputation and well-being without ever doing anything *actually* illegal. So when Facebook started taking down the Russian troll farms' news pages, they said, 'You're attacking our freedom of speech.' So freedom of speech has been turned against the values that it was meant to support.

How you deal with it is a huge question. It would be disastrous to start introducing censorship – that means we roll back 1989. Putin doesn't mind if we introduce censorship – then he'll just do more as well, and so will the Chinese. So we can't suddenly start talking like censors and we've started to do that. The regulation in Europe that's coming out around the internet is all framed as, 'We've got to stop the disinformation.' Disinformation isn't a legal term.

So we have to make sense of what the democratic rules of the information space are. That's a huge project but I would start with thinking about the rights of the person online. At the moment we're a bit like Caliban on Prospero's island, surrounded by bots, trolls, algorithms, and we don't understand how the information environment is being shaped.

And we're kind of made to feel and fear things. Television was manipulative, but we knew that – 'It's a television station owned by Murdoch therefore I can criticize it thus.' We had a relationship with all this power around us and now we don't know what the hell is going on.

Peter Pomerantsev: I wouldn't regulate against content; I would regulate toward transparency. I would regulate so we'd start to understand how the environments around this are shaped.

Andrew Keen: And the third area?

Peter Pomerantsev: The third one is the ideological one, because behind the technological crisis is the ideological one.

Andrew Keen: Behind or they're both sort of there and they're kind of feeding each other?

Peter Pomerantsev: Yeah, it's an intertwined relationship.

Andrew Keen: And the ideological conflict is one of a post-modernist denial of the idea of truth versus the idea of expertise and facts?

Peter Pomerantsev: Which I think is in turn a subset of this idea of the loss of a rational future, not just a dreamy, unrealistic future but a concrete one.

Andrew Keen: So ultimately won't the solution come with a new generation of politicians who are able to tap public disillusionment with this system, as perhaps is happening now in Russia, that might be happening in Turkey, that may conceivably happen in the United States in 2020? At what point will the people get sick of all these lies and of a world of propaganda?

Peter Pomerantsev: Well, let's look at the historical record on this. It's not like we haven't been here before.

Andrew Keen: When were we here before?

Peter Pomerantsev: With the introduction of print.

Andrew Keen: Well, that was 500 years ago.

Peter Pomerantsev: Yes, but then you have the Wars of Religion…

Andrew Keen: So do we have to go through all that? A 30-year war? Is it going to be that bad?

Peter Pomerantsev: Firstly, I think that actually the casualties might not be here and I think casualties are already happening in places like Syria. I think that's part of this same crisis.

ECE TEMELKURAN

What is the process that leads a country to slide from democracy into dictatorship? For an answer, I flew to Zagreb where the distinguished Turkish columnist and writer Ece Temelkuran, author of *How to Lose a Country: The Seven Steps from Democracy to Dictatorship*, is in self-imposed exile from Erdogan's Turkey.

The 'country' in Ece's book isn't just Turkey: it's also Maria Ressa's Philippines; it's the Russia that Peter Pomerantsev understands so well; and it's Doug Rushkoff and Eli Pariser's America. Ece's guide to the seven steps is also a warning about the slow, yet seemingly inevitable, slide into twenty-first-century neo-authoritarianism. It's also a particularly important warning of the risk of falling under the spell of what she describes as 'the real people' – the corrosive and divisive weapon of 'yesterday' populist politicians like Putin, Erdogan, and Trump.

Andrew Keen: Ece Temelkuran, you've written a new book *How to Lose a Country: The Seven Steps from Democracy to Dictatorship*. You're a Turkish journalist now living in exile in Zagreb in Croatia. It's a very personal narrative; it's not an academic book. You have a huge social media following in Turkey and some of your fiction has won awards, but not everyone will know who you are. Who is Ece Temelkuran?

Ece Temelkuran: That's a very profound question. Very briefly, I was a journalist in Turkey for 20 years and published literary books as well. Some of my books are published in English and in other European languages but I'm quite new in the United States. A novel of mine, *The Time of Mute Swans*, was published two years ago, and now *How to Lose a Country* will be my second book published in the United States.

I'm living in Zagreb. I'm not an exile – I don't like to call myself like that – but obviously I am here due to the fact that Turkey is going through some interesting times. Yeah, that's the small version I think of who is Ece Temelkuran.

Andrew Keen: Are you in Croatia because you would be put in prison if you lived in Turkey? Do you fear for your personal safety or are you just more comfortable now living out of Turkey?

Ece Temelkuran: The word 'exile' is something I reject because it brings this emotional and political baggage that I am not willing to carry on my shoulders. I've lived in several countries – in Tunisia, in Lebanon, in Paris, in Oxford, and I tried to see this period of my life as another, when I am writing books and I am away from home.

My life has always been split in between two words, road and home, and I try to see this period as one of those times. I wouldn't say that I would be in prison automatically, but the unpredictability of the political situation in Turkey for people like me is quite exhausting and gives me no time or space to concentrate on any kind of intellectual world. And you will see this in the United States as well – when the political sphere is terrorized to a certain degree, the subtlety of the intellectual word vanishes. When polarization takes over it becomes 'yes' and 'no' and unfortunately the intellectual word takes place in between these two words, and that is quite impossible in Turkey at this point.

Andrew Keen: In your book you have this wonderful term 'real people'. I don't know if any of your 'real people' listen to this show, but if they do they will be thinking, 'This Ece is just another example of a kind of international intellectual elite. She's got her fancy book deals. She's a non-fiction writer. She's got a book launched in the United States. She lives in North Africa and Croatia and the United States. What does she know about the struggle to put food on the table and feed a family?' How would you respond to the critique of Ece from the 'real person'?

Ece Temelkuran: Actually, last weekend I was in Sydney and I was saying to a friend that if somebody ever says I'm part of a cosmopolitan elite, I'm going to rub this economy class boarding pass in his face.

Andrew Keen: So you mean you're not part of the elite because you still travel economy class to Sydney? You still go to Sydney though – that's pretty fancy.

Ece Temelkuran: Besides the joke, we should be very careful about this polarization that is imposed by right-wing populists, that of the oppressive elite and the real people. In the beginning, this 'elite' depends on a class issue, a financial situation, or being able to travel around the world and so on. But as time goes by, as the right-wing populist leader sees more and more power, the parameters change. And then, at the end of the day, it comes to *obedience*. If you're obedient to the leader, you are a member of the real people and if you're not obedient, even if you are poor or undereducated, you are still an elite. I tried to explain how that transformed in Turkey, that divide of elite and real people, and I am seeing the same things happening in Europe and the United States as well.

I think we should be rejecting the divide entirely – otherwise it becomes unbeatable as the right-wing populism gathers more political power.

Andrew Keen: Is the country in your title *How to Lose a Country* really Turkey or is it everywhere?

Ece Temelkuran: It is everywhere and one of the reactions I get for the book as I'm launching it in several languages in Europe is that people tell me they feel less alone. I've heard this in the Netherlands, in Paris, in Germany, everywhere I launch the book – even in Sydney in fact. I think people feel the same things that I felt ten years ago in Turkey and I wrote the book for them, so they don't waste all the time that we lost in Turkey and get their shit together to defend the democracies that they are living in and that they have taken for granted for such a long time, and also so that they notice the moral decay that they are witnessing at the moment, alongside the political insanity...

With the book, I tried to come up with the common global patterns of right-wing populism – how the logic works and how the main mechanism of right-wing populism works, despite the fact that every country has unique conditions. It is only natural to say that every country is different, but there is a common pattern that operates in exactly the same way in every country, even though those countries are completely different demographically, in terms of history and so on.

And at the end it comes to deciding to defend the representative democracy or not. And when it comes to that point, no country is different from the other and no democracy is more immune to right-wing populism than the others. Sometimes this sounds quite absurd to those people who think that the maturity of democracy and the strength of state institutions will protect them from right-wing populism, but as far as I have observed in recent years, democracies and societies respond to right-wing populism almost in the same way – with excess of emotion, being outraged, shocked, surprised, appalled and so on, and then without even noticing they fall into the game of right-wing populism. I wanted to decipher this game of populism for those people who are too confident in their own country's strengths or their democracy's maturity.

Andrew Keen: The subtitle of the book is *The Seven Steps from Democracy to Dictatorship*, which sounds like a Hitchcock movie. Lay out those steps very briefly; what are those seven steps?

Ece Temelkuran: The first step is to create a movement and establish this movement upon the real people, which would be very familiar with Europeans and Americans at the moment. And then ask for respect and get yourself recognized by conventional politics and get yourself a place at that table of conventional politics and then terrorize the political space, so everybody gets really mad or surprised and appalled.

Andrew Keen: So this is an Orbán, a Salvini, a Trump, an Erdogan, right?

Ece Temelkuran: Exactly. As soon as you give them a place at the table of conventional politics, they elbow you out from that table.

Andrew Keen: Right.

Ece Temelkuran: The second step is to disrupt rationale and terrorize the language. I wrote a fictitious conversation between Aristotle and a typical right-wing populist in that chapter to show people how they shouldn't talk to a right-wing populist spin doctor.

The third step is to remove shame: immorality is the new black. I do think that what we are going through is not only a political chaos but a moral one as well, so we have to defend the basic humane, moral values while we're trying to get over this political madness.

Andrew Keen: It seems like the crown prince of this, if that's the right word, is Vladimir Putin and this disappearance of morality.

Ece Temelkuran: That is very interesting, because all these leaders, as I write in the book, are respecting Putin and Putin is respecting them back. So there's an international respect network among these leaders. They are copying each other, because they're so limited in their creativity that they are taking the slogan from each other: 'Make your country great again'.

Andrew Keen: And maybe some of these people have just been watching too many episodes of *The Sopranos* or *Goodfellas* or *The Godfather*?

Ece Temelkuran: Exactly. I'm now reading *Bibi*, a biography of Benjamin Netanyahu by Anshel Pfeffer, an amazing book. And I'm now thinking that before Putin there was Netanyahu. Real people, elites, divine as well.

Andrew Keen: Okay; so number four?

Ece Temelkuran: The fourth step is to dismantle the judiciary and political mechanism. This happened in the United States before anything else, which was very interesting. The United States jumped from first step to fourth step when Trump started to mess with the state institutions.

Andrew Keen: Isn't this a little over-dramatized? I know Trump wants to dismantle the judiciary, but I'm talking to you from Berkeley, California, and there doesn't seem to me at this point much evidence that the judiciary has been dismantled or that he's had any success at all. Where is your evidence for that?

Ece Temelkuran: He's meddling with it, and that was quite unthinkable five years ago, wasn't it? And now it's becoming normalized that he's moving state officials from here to there, he's hiring people and then getting other people that he finds great, and so on.

My point is not that there has been a complete dismantlement of the state institution, but that as soon as the leader starts meddling with the state institution in the eyes of the people, it becomes something like a paper tiger. Probably many people in the United States think, 'Oh, wow – the CIA or FBI were not as strong as we imagined them.'

But Congress had to come together to stop him doing things. The government shutdown, the longest in American history, happened and in order to stop it the entire American establishment had to come together. These are new things so, bit by bit, it becomes normalized that state institutions can be meddled with.

This is how it started in Turkey as well. It didn't happen overnight that the entire political and judiciary mechanism was dismantled; it started with this normalization. The threshold of impossibility became higher as the days went by. So I am calling on people to be careful about this normalization, but when you say Trump couldn't do it, it's an interesting statement – he tried and he did it up to a certain point and then somebody stopped him. So if he did these things on a daily basis, would there be enough political energy to stop him each time?

Andrew Keen: Okay, so number five, the fifth step?

Ece Temelkuran: Number five is something I like very much – it is about political humor. When does laughter become such a comfortable political shelter that we don't want to go out? As soon as these political leaders appear, we start making jokes about them and mock them – it's a defense mechanism to calm down our anxieties. And we use them to feel strong and powerful against this wave of right-wing populism, but then it becomes a tool to make ourselves feel secure even when we're not.

So how does political humor operate in times of rising right-wing populism? That's the fifth step. And the sixth is to design your own citizen. If we let right-wing populism stay in the power long enough, as we did in Turkey, they create their own generation and also harvest people from other political stances to act together with them so they are in fact designing their own citizens. And then people like me feel like they are not citizens anymore.

The last step is to design your own country and get rid of all the others, all the ones who do not support you. This is the saddest phase that I want no European country, or the United States, to face.

Andrew Keen: Let's go back to the second one, which I think is particularly interesting – this idea of the crisis of terrorizing language. Is that why writers like yourself are so important?

Ece Temelkuran: Well, I don't feel important.

Andrew Keen: Well, you're fighting back. The obvious question is that these steps aren't inevitable and the issue is how to push back against them, how to save democracy? And as a writer, I assume that your role is fighting back against the linguistic terrorism.

Ece Temelkuran: Exactly. When the power is primitive, the opposition becomes primitive accordingly. For instance, there was a case in Turkey when it was revealed that in a religious foundation dozens of kids were raped. And this religious foundation was supportive of Erdogan, so therefore he supported this religious foundation and they prosecuted the reporter who reported these rape cases.

So all of a sudden, as opposition we found ourselves saying, 'Raping kids is not good.' I'm a lawyer by education and I've written several books and my intellectual capacity is far better than saying that, but in a country like that you're obliged to repeat this every day. This somehow paralyzes your mind. The power makes you primitive and it's a very annoying and exhausting thing.

There is not subtlety there; there is no sophistication at all. Your brain wants to do something that it is designed for, which is thinking, analyzing and so on. So it was almost like an intellectual reflex for me to start seeing right-wing populism as a giant machine and that is why I wanted to decipher its mechanism. If you're lost in that mechanism you find yourself just shouting, 'No, no, no, no', which doesn't require a lot of intellectual capacity. And it strips you of your intellectual and emotional capabilities; you become this angry person and anger becomes the most defining aspect of your soul.

It is something that the people of Turkey know very well – they are exhausted of being angry and of their language being terrorized and their rationale being disrupted.

It's easier now to explain what happened in Turkey in the last ten years because the Europeans and Americans have something similar. We had to talk to these people who believe that the world is flat and when we showed them the picture of the planet and it's round, they told us, 'But we believe it's flat.' So we have to prove to them that seeing is more valid than believing.

So it becomes like a conundrum that you cannot get out of and you are constantly subjected to this mobilized and politicized ignorance. It's not easy to survive, and throughout that time the most important thing you find out is that the language you're using is terrorized as well – this is what I mean by 'terrorizing the language and disrupting the rationale'.

Andrew Keen: You say that the banality of evil is being replaced by the evil of banality at one point in the book.

Ece Temelkuran: Exactly, and I think this is an important transformation. We thought that all this banality was funny, but then that banality became the president of the United

States. That banality has become significant political leaders and now they are ruining the entire ideal of Europe. So it is not just banal; we are dealing with the evil of banality.

CATHERINE FIESCHI

I first met Catherine Fieschi in 2018 at an event about the crisis of contemporary democracy in Paris. Her book, *Populocracy: The Tyranny of Authenticity and the Rise of Populism,* does an impressive job of explaining the rise of twenty-first-century populism, and when we met again in London in September 2019 she outlined the major characteristics of populism.

As Catherine explained, it's no coincidence that populism has become a dominant force in a digital age in which expertise has been disintermediated and the media has been radically democratized. But as much as the internet has triggered the rise of populist movements around the world, she also believes that 'big data' can provide leaders with the resources to solve complex political problems. The politicians of tomorrow, Catherine suggests, have to rebuild the idea of expertise by taking advantage of technology rather than fighting against it.

Andrew Keen: Catherine Fieschi, just when we thought democracy was finished, you come out with a book called *Populocracy* – so the masses have won, is that the message of your book?

Catherine Fieschi: I think the overall message is that the populist challenge is very much in the democratic tradition; it's just a democratic tradition that we don't particularly want or particularly like. It's heavily majoritarian, it's suppressive, it's unkind to minorities and so in many respects it's not the kind of democracy we want for diverse societies. It's not fit for purpose for that.

And the reason I say 'populocracy' is that it is definitely one of the dominant forms of political expression at the moment across the world – this reference to 'the people' is a constant, almost everywhere we look.

Andrew Keen: But isn't that what democracy is?

Catherine Fieschi: Well, this is why I think it's been so difficult for those of us who were relatively critical of populism to address it in constructive ways, because it's very hard to stand up as a democrat and say we don't like you, we don't like your form of democracy.

As I said, it's a democracy that basically argues that the will of the majority is everything. Even if you have a very large minority, and Brexit is a case in point, where essentially 52 per cent of the people have spoken, that seems to be enough in this what I would call 'populocracy' to wipe out the opinions, the votes, the interests, and the desires of 48 per cent of the population.

So it's a very particular kind of democracy, but it's true that in some ways they've stolen some of the best tunes about 'the popular will', about people being able to make decisions as 'sovereign' and so on and so forth, and I think it's put a lot of us on the back foot in terms of how to argue back.

Andrew Keen: What are the intellectual origins of 'populocracy'? As with democracy, can we trace it back to the Greeks, or is it something more modern about its origins?

Catherine Fieschi: I think that to some extent the populism that I'm interested in, the kind of 'populocracy' that I refer to, is something that is modern in the sense that I think it is a hallmark of advanced democracies, because to some extent I would argue that populocracy and populist politics are a reaction from people in places where there has been a real democratic promise and where that democratic promise is seen to be broken.

So whether it's continuous improvement for the middle classes or whether it's ever-increasing prosperity and so on and so forth – these are things that often go hand in hand with mature democracies. When they are seen to be stalling, this is partly when the kind of populism that I'm talking about tends to emerge. So I would argue that it's a modern form of politics.

I think that in terms of our democratic tradition and how we've got to where we are, there's a confluence of things that is interesting. One is that we're living at a time where the digital transformation and digital revolution has created some very valuable tools, but also I think some very pernicious illusions about our capacity to express ourselves very directly with one another, our capacity to understand very quickly; it's kind of eradicated any sense that actually some things are very complex and cannot be boiled down to 140 or 280 characters.

Andrew Keen: So in terms of your narrative of populocracy, you would date it back to the beginnings of the internet? Is it any coincidence that we seem to have the rise of these populist, charismatic leaders over the last 30 years, just as the digital revolution has transformed society?

Catherine Fieschi: I think that this isn't a coincidence. I don't want to lay everything at the doorstep of digital or social media, but I do think that the transformation of the media and the impact that they've had in terms of what we want from politics, the way we conceive of our relationship, both to one another and to the political realm, I think that this has been an exponential boost to populism because it goes hand in hand with the populist promise that is to say, 'We understand everything that you're about. We understand you deeply and instinctively and we will deliver very quickly what everyone else is telling you. This whole story that things are complex, they're just bamboozling you. We know that actually it boils down to some simple things.' Unfortunately, I think that's something that social media and the digital revolution has heightened – the power of that message of simplicity and ease and transparency.

Andrew Keen: So what do all populists have in common? Is it an anti-elitism, an anti-establishmentism?

Catherine Fieschi: I think it's definitely an anti-elitism and an anti-establishmentism.

Andrew Keen: And it's a hostility to experts and expertise and learning?

Catherine Fieschi: A hostility to experts, to expertise, to learning, to discernment, the idea that there are grey areas, but this is a very Manichean view of the world, that it's black and white. And I think that in that respect, all populists have that in common and they all have in common this sense that the people, however they want to be defined, are the repository of morality and common sense, and that that makes them infinitely superior to those people who have book smarts or expertise or any of the appanage of the elite.

Andrew Keen: So how do you fight populism?

Catherine Fieschi: In the book, one of my points is that populism has done a jujitsu on us democrats. It's taken democracy and it's flipped it around and has hit us over the head with it, and we haven't been able to react very well.

And so what's the jujitsu move we do back? And I think it's about actually not letting them colonize that idea of authenticity and take it over for themselves, that idea that they understand these voters in a way that no one else can. Actually, I know that for some this is a conclusion that seems a bit weak, but my advice is that what we've done so far is we've tinkered on the edges with policy and we've basically had these mealy-mouthed apologies about how we're going to do better and how we're going to cap immigration. I don't think that that's the answer. I think that we have at our disposal infinitely fine-grained and granular information about where the pockets of need are, about what people truly are missing in terms of education, in terms of care, in terms of being included. The beauty of big data is not that it's big; the beauty of big data is that it's granular.

Andrew Keen: So you're saying the solution to the contempt for the experts is more expertise?

Catherine Fieschi: I think it's showing that we know how to *use* that expertise in a way that matters to people. I think one of the reasons that people have switched off from it is that expertise has been caricatured as being told you can eat one thing one day but you can't eat it the next day, scientists disagreeing and so on. That's what I think a lot of ordinary people think expertise is, and it gets in their way of leading their lives.

How about using the tools that we've got in order to produce an expertise that actually visibly meets the needs that they have? Because when the populists turn around and say, 'We really understand you,' the fact is they don't. But might we be able to turn around and say, 'Actually here's what we're going to do. We're really going to bring this in. We're really going to address some of these issues that we've got, because we do have the information that we need to do that.'

IAN BREMMER

I first met Ian Bremmer, one of America's most formidable conversationalists, when we were on opposite sides of a formal debate titled 'Automation will crash democracy'. Ian, who was arguing in favor of the motion, crushed me – as he does all his debate opponents. Not only is he a masterful orator who is able to convincingly present any side of any argument – he's also a skilled listener who can pick up on the nuance of other people's ideas.

But there's more to Ian than intellectual showmanship. As he argued in this interview, the contemporary crisis of democracy hasn't been caused only by automation or any other kind of smart digital technology. The real issue is a human one: we've lost the ability to talk to people of different opinions. So while the fact that our culture resembles an echo chamber is obviously related to technology, there is no technological fix that enables us to become better conversationalists. A healthy democracy requires conversationalists who are skilled in not just talking but also listening. It needs more people like Ian Bremmer.

Andrew Keen: Ian Bremmer, the author of *Us vs Them: The Failure of Globalism*; has globalism really failed? That's a pretty outrageous statement, especially for a global strategist like you to make.

Ian Bremmer: Globalization is this idea that open borders and free trade and global security provided by the US and its allies is good for the global economy, and that's obviously true. We've seen extraordinary growth in the period of globalization and we've taken over a billion people out of absolute poverty. We're educating people. We're driving urbanization. It's certainly bad for the climate, and that's a serious issue, but if you look at the human condition, people are getting immunized, becoming literate, and getting access to proper healthcare, and that's a great thing.

Andrew Keen: Last week we had Soli Ozel, the Turkish political pundit on, who argued that the two key problems about democracy are fixing capitalism and regulating big tech, but do you believe that the failure of globalism has essentially undermined democracy because the things you brought up – Brexit, the Yellow Jackets in France – aren't those manifestations of democracy working?

Ian Bremmer: Well sure, insofar as you have angry people expressing that anger in legitimate political ways and not actually trying to tear down the system. So I think the fact that there are referenda and democratic elections that continue to work shows that democracy is functioning.

Andrew Keen: In your book you have a really intriguing introduction where you suggest that more and more people in the world are like Palestinians, in the sense that voting isn't helping them, so they spend their lives throwing rocks. Do you want to develop that metaphor of more and more people finding themselves in the dilemma of the Palestinians?

Ian Bremmer: It's a depressing analogy but more and more people are becoming like the Palestinians in two ways. First of all, because we don't care about them; we have a world where information cycles immediately. We know what the Palestinians are going through. In Gaza you've got 50 per cent unemployment, you've got 40 per cent of people not getting enough to eat, you've got no educational prospects or employment prospects for these people or their kids, and yet, whether it's the United States or the Europeans or the Israelis or even the Palestinian Authority, they're not really doing anything for these people and the people feel that way.

So first of all, you have the fact that nobody cares, and secondly you have the fact that they're feeling powerlessness and helplessness, and that means that increasingly not only are they throwing rocks at the Israel Defense Forces, but they're even throwing themselves at the border which is defended by

Israeli troops who have orders to use lethal force for anyone approaching that border and trying to breach it. A number of Palestinians have been killed, and that shows an extraordinary level of discontent with the people that have been lying to them for decades saying, 'Oh, we're going to take care of you, we're going to ensure there's a Two-State Solution and we're going to get you economic capacity to improve yourselves.' It just hasn't happened, and I think that if you look at what's happened to a lot of people living in our countries in the West, they increasingly feel like they're being lied to and that nobody cares about them. And that's why they're suddenly either not voting at all or voting for an awful lot of people that are well outside the traditional norms of what we consider to be a polite political society.

Andrew Keen: So are you suggesting, then, that the working classes of Western Europe or the United States, the people who are struggling to find a place for themselves in the globalized economy, that they are like the Palestinians, that they've come to throwing rocks? And are you suggesting that voting for Brexit or for Trump or for Bolsonaro or Erdogan is like throwing rocks?

Ian Bremmer: I am, and I'll tell you why: it's because when you throw a rock, you don't believe that that's actually going to improve your situation. You run after you throw it, so it's not like you think it's a win, but it does give you a voice and actually shows that you're not going to sit down and just take it. You're still an independent human being and you can't be treated that way without a response.

And I think that all the people that voted for Brexit, I don't think they all actually thought Brexit was going to improve their lives, but they did believe the system was rigged against them and that all the people with their fancy educations were telling them why they shouldn't vote for Brexit, so they voted for Brexit.

I think in the United States a vote for Trump was a thumb in the eye of polite society. Trump's willingness to go after the mainstream media is something that a lot of those supporters really believe in – his going after a lot of the globalist elites and saying that he's going to drain the swamp, even though he's not actually doing it, which is the sad thing. But I do think that they are very similar and these are people who believe that the system is rigged against them.

Andrew Keen: And are you suggesting then that what we call democracy is increasingly an aristocracy of well-educated, globalized people like you and me?

Ian Bremmer: It certainly feels that way. In the United States especially there is nowhere close to the level of class mobility that you had in the 1970s and 1980s. In the United States among all the advanced industrial economies, it's easier to judge what the wealth of a child will be on the basis of how wealthy the parents are. Now that's something we used to think of as not applying to the US – we thought it applied more to the UK or Germany or the Netherlands or France, but actually no, it applies to the United States and that does feel like a subversion of the American dream. It feels like a subversion of a country with elected representatives that are supposed to actually work for the people as opposed to working for special interests who pay them a lot of money.

Andrew Keen: And in your book you're suggesting that this situation is going to get even worse with automation, with the way in which AI will radically transform the economy? So if your message isn't already depressing, it becomes even more pessimistic. Is that fair?

Ian Bremmer: Well, it's a mixed message. You asked me at the beginning what I think about globalization and I said I'm in favor. What do I think about AI? I'm in favor because I believe that artificial intelligence is going to create enormous sufficiencies and enormous wealth, but it's only going to work for the average person if it's properly regulated, if we have a social contract that's effective, if we're retraining and reskilling these people and doing so over the course of their lives and not just the first 16 or 18 or 22 years of it. We're not doing that right now and we have no political leaders in place that are credibly talking about how we might get from here to there.

So yes, I do think that for the near-term future, the next five, ten years, we're going to go through a pretty tough patch, where a lot of people are going to find that the system is working against them and the faster contributions of technology to make us wealthier are things that they are not benefiting from.

Andrew Keen: In your book, you also talk about the rewriting of the social contract. Does that rewriting happen within the formal institutions of democracy? Is it a political movement? How do we rewrite our social contract in the early twenty-first century to make democracy more inclusive, or to at least guard ourselves against this creeping aristocratic structure of society?

Ian Bremmer: Well, the last time we did it was after the Great Depression. It was FDR and it was the New Deal, and that's when we put social security in place and suddenly dramatically changed the regulatory environment for big corporations. And there was a lot of wealth redistribution.

I don't think we're anywhere near that level of urgency in the United States. The poor in the US are a lot wealthier today even than they were during the Great Depression, and so it doesn't feel very urgent.

Andrew Keen: You're quite dramatic in the way in which you see this crisis. You say that day is coming sooner than we think, in terms of the need to rewrite this social contract. This is not a minor issue.

Ian Bremmer: It's not a minor issue, but the reason I say that we're like the Palestinians is if you think about 20 to 30 years ago and all the op-eds that were written about how we needed to fix this or Israel is going to fall apart, it turns out it's not true. Israel just had an election a month ago and the Palestinians weren't even a part of it. Neither of the two candidates for premier, Netanyahu or Benny Gantz, were talking about needing to address the Palestinian issue.

It's not urgent for the Israelis, so while you have a whole bunch of people getting angrier and angrier in the United States, the fact is that there's very little perceived need for the government and for the people in power to do more than a box-checking exercise. Alexandria Ocasio-Cortez can certainly talk about a 'Green New Deal', but nobody that has real power right now is credibly moving in that direction.

So I think that the solutions we're talking about are going to be piecemeal, they're going to be small, they're going to be experimental. Some will come from mayors and governors; some will come from CEOs and individual philanthropists and over time hopefully we'll scale them, but realistically speaking this is going to get worse before it gets better. It's kind of the geopolitical equivalent of climate change: if you'd asked me about climate change 30 or 40 years ago and I had the science at my fingertips, I would tell you that this is getting worse but we're clearly not getting ready to fix it any time soon. We have to get through the point of awareness by people that really matter and start putting resources toward it. And that is not on today's agenda.

Andrew Keen: Yes, I get your point now about the Palestinians as being a kind of political theater that doesn't matter; that they throw rocks, sometimes gets in the headlines, it makes them feel better, but nothing changes. But what about institutional changes within democracy itself? In Ireland, for example, they're experimenting with 'Citizen Committees' that can fix stuff that referenda usually aren't able to address in a serious way. Should we be thinking about formal reform to the kind of institutional nature of twenty-first-century democracy? Can it be distributed? Can it be radically reformed?

Ian Bremmer: It's easier in small countries that are homogeneous and can be much more quickly responsive to populations that they know and can touch. That's why I said that in the United States I think you're talking more about cities and governors of small states than you are talking about reforming Washington as a whole.

When you talk about Washington, you're talking about needing to remove money from politics. You're talking about some basic structural reforms that are very hard to implement, but when you're talking about smaller countries like Finland, which is dealing with AI by putting cash to ensure that 1 per cent of the entire population is educated about AI so they can build a civil society that is focused on these sorts of issues, I love that as an experiment. I think that's a smart thing to do, but it's really hard to make that happen on a countrywide basis in the world's largest economy, the United States.

Andrew Keen: Ian, what about the role of social media and the digital revolution in all this? Do you think, given your metaphor of the Palestinians, that fixing fake news, and addressing all the problems associated with social media might reduce the rock-throwing?

Ian Bremmer: Absolutely. There's no question in my mind that what you have seen with social media is the weaponizing of inequality because it really does polarize society into not engaging with people with different views, only talking to people they already agree with, being much more susceptible to radicalization, to extreme political movements, and to fake news being propagated by those that seek to profit and benefit from attracting more people to narrower perspectives. We need to do something about that.

I think that Facebook, Twitter, and YouTube should come with a warning label that says, 'Use as directed will be hazardous to your health.'

Andrew Keen: Like tobacco?

Ian Bremmer: Absolutely. It's very clear that these companies are bad for human beings, as their business model necessarily productizes people in ways that are fundamentally unhealthy and need to be regulated. The problem is that the alternative to those companies right now globally are Chinese companies that are very effective, have a lot more data, and are actively supported by their government. If we're going to regulate and undermine the profitability of some of our most important industrial companies that are critical for our economy and our national security while the Chinese are only investing in them to make them stronger, that may be good for near-term civic harmony in the US, but we may be undermining our national security against our most important antagonist globally.

I don't have an answer for that, but I think we need to be talking about it. I'm deeply concerned about this.

Andrew Keen: You bring up China. I know you're quite an authority on China. Are they constructing a viable alternative to Western democracy, with their social credit system and the way in which they're using digital technology to rebuild a more effective *1984* in the twenty-first century?

Ian Bremmer: They seem to be. Even if we think it's not going to work very well long term, and I think the jury is still out, the fact is that they are very likely to become the largest economy in the world, surpassing the US, in the next ten years. They are spending a hell of a lot more outside their country on infrastructure and other enticements than the Americans are. Money talks, and a viable model that includes writing checks to you seems suddenly a lot more attractive, even if you might prefer the American alternative. And you asked about social credit; it's clear that technology and big data and the surveillance that comes with being able to collect and manipulate that effectively is allowing the Chinese government to steer the behavior of its populations and its companies in directions that strengthen an authoritarian Chinese system.

That worries me greatly. It certainly has facilitated the imprisonment of over 1 million Muslim Uyghurs living inside China, who are seen to be potential threats to Chinese behavior and with barely a peep in terms of internal dissent. I think that's a serious concern. If you're American or if you're living in any Western democracy and are hopeful about the viability of our system long term, you have to be deeply concerned about what the Chinese are doing today.

Andrew Keen: All this is extremely chilling. We're becoming Palestinians. The Chinese are constructing a totalitarian alternative to a Western democratic system that isn't working. Let's spend the rest of this conversation focusing on concrete fixes. Give me some ways that we can begin to fix the problems that globalism has created in Western democracies. Actual initiatives. I understand that there are no quick fixes, but things that will begin to address these issues.

Ian Bremmer: Well an obvious one would be in a low-interest rate environment. We need to be spending an awful lot more on infrastructure to improve the lives of the people that feel like the system is rigged against them, so that means real spending on improved local infrastructure in rural areas and second- and third-tier cities. It means going after the teachers' unions and spending locally and statewide on improved early stage education, focusing not just on the vocational schools but instead taking advantage of AI and teaching more critical thinking, teaching more curiosity, creating more dilettantism, people that will have the ability to be more flexible with their jobs over the course of decades.

Andrew Keen: Finally Ian, not everyone listening to this will be part of the global elite. What can ordinary people do to help fix this? Everyone will say, 'Well, I'm relying on government, I'm relying on this candidate or that candidate or trillions of dollars being invested in infrastructure,' but as you suggested we can't all just pass the buck. What can everyday people do to begin to address this issue? Do they need to check their psychology? Do they need to rethink their role in the world?

Ian Bremmer: I think that the average person needs to do what they can to break down this very dehumanizing process that has been built up by the business models of social media that's driving us crazy about politics. We need to become 10 per cent less crazy, 10 per cent less angry, and one way to do that is to make sure that you are actually actively listening to, following and engaging with people that you respect but disagree with.

Any person out there listening to this, I ask are there people out there that you can think of that you think are really smart but you fundamentally disagree with on some political issues? If you can't come up with four or five of those people, then you've got a serious problem – that means that you're following the mandate of these companies, these algorithms that are creating a prison for your mind that you cannot see. It's very *Matrix*-like. And you've got to break out of that. You have to actually proactively find and follow and engage with the people who are smart that make you think. And the food companies back in the 1970s and 1980s were giving us the food that we said we wanted, but in reality they just wanted to sell us more; it was all the fat, all the salty, all the sweet, and within 20 years we had the highest type 2 diabetes and obesity in the world.

I blame the companies for that and I blame the government for not properly regulating them, but until we get proper regulation and the companies change their business models, we as consumers have to try to use these products more responsibly. The companies are not going to help us. They don't care about us. They're making us into products, and we have to fight back.

MARTIN WOLF

Martin Wolf, chief economics commentator of the *Financial Times*, has always seemed to understand the science of economics better than mortals like you and me, so I was thrilled to find myself on the 2018 Global Peter Drucker Forum panel with him in Vienna, discussing the crisis of democracy.

Wolf fears the impact of technology: 'When [it] knows everything about every one of us, is that the end of democracy?' he suggested to the audience. He articulated a similar fear in his conversation with me, and when economists of his stature suggest that surveillance capitalism could kill democracy, we should take note. And Wolf's warning from the heart of old Europe, which is now experiencing its own profound crisis of democracy, is particularly chilling. But for all his warnings about the dangers of surveillance capitalism, he remains in the 'tomorrow' camp. We need to invent new political parties and ideologies, he reminds us, and to move forward with innovative ideas rather than being seduced by the nostalgia of the 'yesterdays'.

Andrew Keen: Martin, you're an economist who likes writing about politics, so what is the role of economics, particularly globalization, in today's crisis of democracy?

Martin Wolf: I think that's an absolutely fundamental question. I've always felt, by the way, partly because of my background and my education, that politics and economics are twins. The idea that you can consider the economy without paying attention to politics strikes me as incredibly naive.

My answer to your question of what role does globalization play, I think one has to divide it in two completely different ways. First of all, what does it do in reality as opposed to how it is perceived? And there's no doubt at all that people are aware of and sensitive to the impact of things foreigners do or the presence of foreigners, often out of proportion to their actually economic significance, because we are tribal.

The globalization, and I'm here thinking about trade, about migration, which is a form of globalization, is perceived as having a much greater impact on people than it really does, but that's to be expected because of who we are.

The second way of cutting this is by the different aspects of globalization, so there's trade, there's the movement of capital, there's the movement of people, and there's the movement of ideas. These are related, but they are different. I think the evidence to my mind, which is quite surprising, is that trade itself has had a significant but actually fairly modest impact on our economies. People have exaggerated this hugely; for example, American politics has recently been blaming imports from China for the loss of the American jobs in factories, but if you go back and look at the statistics carefully you discover it's a fairly modest effect compared to other things.

Capital is a very big deal because it has created a lot of macro-economic instability – financial crisis and so forth – and also there's no doubt that the know-how of Western companies is now available worldwide, has spread knowledge, and made competition globally much fiercer.

Migration is very totemic but economically really quite insignificant. It's not a huge effect but it's *culturally* quite significant. And then there's the globalization of ideas, a lot of which is associated with capital, and of course that is a very profound effect on our society – we've lost our monopoly of knowledge but there's nothing we can do about it. Ideas will move; there's nothing to be done about it.

So in thinking about what globalization has done, I want us to be very rigorous and very careful.

Andrew Keen: Martin, what about the role of global elites in this crisis? You move in the world of Davos, the world of think tanks, and international authorities like you. Are they the solution or the problem?

Martin Wolf: Well, I hope both – and not just the problem. I've made this point before. I've clearly made mistakes in which I was too optimistic about how the new global market economy would operate and insufficiently aware of the dangers, and I think that was generally very true among economists and among advocates of the global economic paradigm, the liberalization paradigm. So I think intellectually we got quite a bit wrong and worse, I think it is clearly true for many of us that we paid too little attention to the interests involved, that we were inevitably creating a paradigm in which very powerful economic interests became increasingly unshackled. And that allowed them to play a political role, which was in significant measure maligned. It allowed them to escape from their public responsibilities; an obvious example of that is all the tax evasion and avoidance that has being going on, and I think that people who were close to the idea of economic liberalization didn't pay enough attention to these downsides and I recognize this as a mistake that people like me have made. We didn't pay enough attention to the political consequences of what we'd been doing, which doesn't mean there are simple solutions because I don't think there are simple solutions, and I don't think that globalization was a huge mistake because it actually did allow for astonishing improvements in economic welfare across the world, but we didn't think about what this would do to our economics, our economies, and our politics, and I'm very frightened about that.

Andrew Keen: What would you make of the arguments of Brexiteers, Trump, and even unabashedly illiberals like Bolsonaro and Erdogan that these are democratic corrections to the problem of global twenty-first century capitalism?

Martin Wolf: They're clearly global reactions, less obvious in the case of Erdogan, except that he got into power in the first place because of the complete failure of the secular elites before him. In the other cases, it's obvious they are reactions, but whether they're corrections depends on what happens now.

Andrew Keen: But are they democratic?

Martin Wolf: They're democratic, but whether they turn out to be corrections depends on what happens now. So in some of these cases, and I think it's pretty obvious in Erdogan's case, it's very unlikely that a democratic process will remove him. In other words, what happens – it's the famous line – you have one man, one vote, once. One man, one vote, once is democratic, but ceases to be democratic afterwards.

To be a democracy politics has to be competitive forever. That's what makes a democracy. So it's only a correction if what happens now is that politics continues to function and if they fail, and I think these people will fail, they can be got rid of democratically. On that we don't know. I'm reasonably optimistic that if Mr Trump loses popularity he can be voted out in America, so that's democracy. In the case of Brexit, of course it's a one-off decision and it can't be easily corrected if it happens, so that's the nature of the decision.

But ultimately, whether these reactions turn into corrections depends on whether the democratic game continues to survive and I think my worry, which is of course linked to what happened in the inter-war period in Europe, is that in some cases democracy is just gone. I think Hungary is another example; I think democracy there is just gone. There is no way under the present constitutional legal arrangements that anyone will unseat Viktor Orbán, and the same is true with Putin in Russia.

Andrew Keen: What exists today that didn't exist in the 1930s is the digital revolution, the internet, artificial intelligence, ubiquitous social media and all its discontents. How do you see the role of all this new technology in today's crisis of democracy?

Martin Wolf: I think that's a really profound question and I'm not sure I've made up my own mind. I think there are two ways of seeing this. The first, which is my optimistic picture, is that using the newspapers, pamphlets, the radio, it was amazing how well they seemed to be able to control public opinion, for example in Nazi Germany. It didn't require modern technology; Hitler won anyway, got to power anyway, he was electorally remarkably successful after the Great Depression, without any of this modern technology, and it's clear that the lie machine was very effective throughout the whole history of Nazi Germany, to the very end. It didn't require modern technology; in that sense, the modern technology is not a necessary condition for this. So that's the optimistic view, if you like, that the new technology is not that important.

But there is a counterargument which is that the manipulation of public opinion with modern technology is much easier and more invisible. It's below the radar. That's what seems to me so striking about the interventions in the recent elections, particularly in the US but also in Brexit, using instruments like Facebook. And of course, not only is that the case, but they can manipulate more effectively because it's more targeted, more personal, cheaper, but of course if all this technology gets into the hands of the state, they can in theory manage and oversee individuals, have surveillance of society down to the individual which those dictators of the past couldn't dream of.

So you have to worry that if such a regime comes into power, it just can't be got rid of, it's there forever. So if that is the case, then these new technologies are sufficiently new to make the nightmares of the twentieth century the realities of the twenty-first.

Andrew Keen: Martin, you use the word 'if', as if it might happen in the future. But isn't this kind of high-tech authoritarianism already being imposed in China?

Martin Wolf: It's not quite clear to me how far it's effectively happened, but there's no doubt at all it's what they're trying to make happen. I think the Chinese Communist Party would be very strong in China even if it didn't have all these technologies, so I'm not saying that it's powerful because of it. The truth is that since the 'Tiananmen incident', as they call it, the Communist Party of China has been remarkably astute. It has managed the economy and the polity really effectively all the way down and I would have thought that it probably continues to have an overwhelming legitimacy anyway, so it doesn't need all this. But yes, it is absolutely clear that they are operating an increasingly pervasive surveillance system as more and more people go online, and the result is that it is difficult to see how anybody could mobilize effectively against them.

That doesn't mean it's over. If you think about how a regime like that ends, think how the Soviet Union ended. It didn't end because of an upwelling of protest from below. It always ends because the regime splits at the top, and the surveillance system will not itself prevent that. What happened in the Soviet Union in the 1980s was that the Community Party of the Soviet Union split profoundly. That seems unlikely to happen now in China, but if China's development stops, and if things start getting really difficult for whatever reason, I think that could happen, and that's why I think that even with this very strong surveillance system over the citizenry, the regime is not necessarily permanently consolidated. But the history will see whether that's right.

Andrew Keen: I'm a little troubled, Martin, by your comment about the legitimacy of this authoritarian Chinese government. Are you suggesting that most Chinese citizens don't want democracy?

Martin Wolf: Well, that's what I'm always told, but of course I haven't spoken to most Chinese people. The Chinese leadership will, of course, always tell you that they'd much rather have stability and prosperity than democracy of which they have no experience and no real idea; it is clear they found – and Xi Jinping himself recognized this – the corruption of the bureaucrats they were dealing with intolerable; and that was very dangerous to the state. So I'm not suggesting at all that they found the regime fully satisfactory and legitimate. All I'm suggesting is that it doesn't seem to me plausible, but I can't prove it because I haven't talked to 1.3 billion Chinese and there's no opinion polls on this in China for obvious reasons.

Andrew Keen: Okay; so we can't control the Chinese government, but we can control our own political systems. Give me a couple of solutions, concrete things that we can do to solve this crisis of democracy.

Martin Wolf: Well the most concrete thing, which applies I think most to the US, is to impose really tight restrictions on the use of money in politics. If politics are for sale in this way then I think we are in terrible trouble.

Andrew Keen: Aren't you sounding a bit like Donald Trump now? 'Clean the swamp…'

Martin Wolf: Well, except that I mean it and he and his party sure don't. Second, I think I have become increasingly tempted by the Australian idea that voting should be compulsory. There are far too many cases when people will not vote and the people who don't vote tend to be the poorer, the less attached to the political process, but these are precisely the people for whom the vote is most significant. So I think there's a very strong case for making voting compulsory.

Third, and this is where it gets complicated, I think there has to be public financing of political parties, so they have the means even without private funding. Because they perform a public role – a political party is providing a public good, it makes a political system work. Now this has to be done without ideological attachment; it could be done in terms of how many votes they get that you give them a certain proportion of public money. In Britain, of course, you have the advantage still but that's diminishing. You can use the BBC and the media as a compulsory way of providing channels for parties to get their messages across, but parties have to be helped. In Germany, parties are given support to do think tanks, to do research on policy and so forth. So support for political parties will be my third element.

Andrew Keen: Martin, without wishing to pigeonhole you, my guess is that politically you're on the center-left.

Martin Wolf: I think of myself as anywhere in between the center-right and the center-left. It wobbles over my life.

Andrew Keen: In America I think you wobble to the left.

Martin Wolf: In America I'm center-left, but in Britain I'm probably center-right actually.

Andrew Keen: So how do we reinvent our center-left? Clearly nobody believes in moderates like Clinton or Blair anymore. My sense is that the traditional European center-left of the industrial age is in retreat. So is a reactionary socialist like Corbyn the inevitable outcome of the crisis of the center-left? Or can a credible moderate, progressive ideology be rebuilt in an age of global capitalism?

Martin Wolf: I think politically that is to me possibly the biggest single question within the systems we're talking about. My answer to that is that I believe you can be radically left of center, significantly more egalitarian than the old 'Third Way' was, while still being strongly pro-market and significantly more interventionist in the economy. I mentioned some very important areas – competition, policy, demonopolization, taking on tax evasion, all the rest of it while still being center-left. But there are some things that the center-left is attached to where I think they're going to have to be much stronger and one of them is they have to make clear that while we're not xenophobic, we are committed to controlling the borders, including over-migration.

I wrote this 15 years ago; it was a great mistake in the US not to let in immigrants but to allow in so many undocumented people. If you lose control of the borders there will be a backlash and so for the center-left I think it's one of those really difficult issues, but I think it's one they have to take on. But what I'm saying is that you can be pro-market but you have to be much more egalitarian, much more interventionist, much more pro-competition, much more determined to remove money from politics and that is a form of center-leftism which I believe could still be popular, and that is certainly the sort of leftism that I would support.

Andrew Keen: Are we going to need a charismatic leftist, a Macron, even though even Macron isn't Macron, a kind of Fabian Churchill?

Martin Wolf: Politics always needs charismatic. Charisma is part of politics and why should the charismatic politicians only be demagogues, populists, and fascists?

Andrew Keen: So where is this progressive charismatic going to come from?

Martin Wolf: Really successful politicians always come from surprising places. So while we can debate his contribution, two years before he emerged nobody expected Barack Obama to emerge from absolutely nowhere. These people will come from wherever they come from. They may be youngsters whom we haven't heard of. I didn't expect Jeremy Corbyn; nobody thought about him, but he's suddenly the most significant charismatic politician in Britain. One always has to hope that in countries with vibrant political traditions, real political leaders will emerge when there is a need, and God knows there's a need.

Andrew Keen: So Martin, you began pessimistically but you've ended on an optimistic note.

Martin Wolf: I've ended hopeful, which is not quite the same thing. Despair is a sin.

PART 4

FIXING THE FUTURE

RICHARD STENGEL

I wasn't quite sure what to expect when I met Richard Stengel in Manhattan in August 2019. In his latest book, *Information Wars: How We Lost the Global Battle Against Disinformation and What We Can Do About It*, Richard – who was Under Secretary of State for Public Diplomacy and Public Affairs in the Obama Administration – described himself, half seriously, as the 'Chief Marketing Officer of the USA', but the only idea he tried to sell me was the role of ideas in the fight against disinformation. The information war against democracy, he insisted, is also a war on truth, so saving the foundation of American democracy, he reasoned, requires a defense of the very idea of truth.

While he acknowledges the role of the digital revolution in the misinformation wars, Richard – who was the editor of *Time* magazine before his stint in the Obama Administration – remains optimistic that the internet could help fix our crisis of democracy. He suggests, for example, that Facebook, one of the primary battlefields of the misinformation war, could potentially become a platform for civic education. Unlike many of the other interviewees in this book, including authorities on Facebook like David Kirkpatrick, Stengel remains cautiously optimistic about the social network. Perhaps it's no surprise that he made Mark Zuckerberg *Time* magazine's Person of the Year in 2010.

Andrew Keen: Richard Stengel, the author of *Information Wars* and the former Chief Marketing Officer of the United States of America, at least that's how you introduce yourself in the book. What did you do as the Chief Marketing Officer of the United States – it's quite a title!

Richard Stengel: It is quite a title, but the real title is Under Secretary of State for Public Diplomacy and Public Affairs, and that basically is the soft power end of government. It's about marketing the USA. That is the traditional nature of the job. The public affairs part is spokespeople and there are spokespeople in every embassy around the world, and in the 1950s it was about marketing America around the world when there was this great competition during the Cold War.

Andrew Keen: Why did you go into government?

Richard Stengel: I believe in public service. In fact, one of the issues I started when I was editor of *Time* was the case for national service. I used to campaign every year for people going and doing some kind of public work. I always knew that I would do it eventually and I had got to the end of my term at *Time*, and I was a very big fan of Barack Obama and they asked me to come in.

Andrew Keen: So, you were the guy doing US soft power and you happened to get involved in politics at a time where

America was dragged into a soft war, the information war. What happened?

Richard Stengel: On this spectrum between soft and hard power, there was an entity that was a hard power entity under me, which was the Center for Strategic Counterterrorism Communications. It was created under Hillary Clinton to combat a terrorist organization called Al Qaeda that was doing dynamic new stuff on the internet. So I got interested in the information war because of that group and because of the rise of ISIS, and then we saw the rise of Russian disinformation at almost the same time – because just as ISIS was coming to the fore, that's when Russia annexed Crimea and we saw this tsunami of disinformation around that.

Andrew Keen: Rick, connect up the crisis of democracy in the West, or at least some of the issues or problems of democracy in the West, with this information war.

Richard Stengel: I'm a kind of American information exceptionalist. Jefferson and the framers believed that for a democracy to work, there needed to be an informed citizenry. The Declaration says that institutions govern among men and women with the consent of the governed. And the consent of the governed is obtained through factual information. Democracies, more than any other system, depend on people being informed.

Andrew Keen: So in your mind, the core of democracy is the free flow of accurate information?

Richard Stengel: The core of democracy is this idea that human beings can govern themselves, and for people to govern themselves they need information to make the wisest decision. And that doesn't even mean that they'll make the wisest decision.

Andrew Keen: So throughout history there's been — and you know this better than I do —misinformation and disinformation. What's so unique about the last 20 years when it comes to these information wars, because throughout history there has been one kind of information war or another?

Richard Stengel: As soon as there was information, there was disinformation. As soon as there was knowledge, there was the misuse of that knowledge. When Satan told Eve that if she took a bite of the apple nothing would happen to her, that was disinformation — and that's the beginning of civilization.

What's different now with the rise of social media is the absolute universality and instantaneousness of this disinformation. Once upon a time, the Russians would have to plant a story in a little newspaper in India and then cover it in the Russian press. Now the smallest tweet can go global almost instantly. What is local is global; and what is global is local, and that's never happened before in human history. That's the transformational change of social media.

Andrew Keen: The internet then?

Richard Stengel: The internet and social media, the universality, the instantaneousness of it is new. People love to quote that Mark Twain line: 'A lie will go round the world while truth is pulling its boots on.' He said that in the nineteenth century, before there was radio.

Andrew Keen: A lot of people trace today's history of democracy from the fall of the Berlin Wall in 1989, but 1989 of course was also the year that Tim Berners-Lee invented the World Wide Web in Geneva. When historians look back at 1989, do you think that the invention of the internet in terms of the challenges and problems of democracy in the twenty-first century will seem more important than the fall of the Wall? Or will these two things be connected?

Richard Stengel: I think they're connected because while Tim Berners-Lee was inventing the internet, there was a KGB officer in Dresden in 1989 looking at the fall of the Berlin Wall and thinking that it had fallen without a single bullet being fired, and without a single missile. The Soviet Union had spent billions and billions of dollars on weaponry and the wall fell because of soft power. That was the lesson that Putin took from the fall of the Berlin Wall. And when he became the head of Russia, he tried to marshal Russia's soft power. He took over the television stations. He basically transformed old-style Soviet active measures into new-style modern Russian disinformation.

Andrew Keen: Is the new Cold War not an ideological conflict, but a conflict about the use and abuse of information?

Richard Stengel: I actually think the information war is bigger than the Cold War. The Cold War was between two different powers with different visions. The information war is a kind of war of all against all. It's a competition among narratives of countries and non-state actors and everybody for the primacy of their view, using disinformation to get to that place. It's a global conflict.

Andrew Keen: In our series we've had an unspoken debate amongst the people we've spoken to about whether or not democracy is really in crisis. Some people say not really; some people say yes. Some people say it's a return to fascism. Looking globally, and not just at Russia and America and the challenge of ISIS, how would you describe the state of democracy in the world today?

Richard Stengel: It's retreating. The number of countries that are considered democracies has been going down for about ten years now. There's a return to 'blood and borders', of countries that want everybody to look like everybody else in the country. They want everyone to have the same heritage and they have these strongmen leaders that are authoritarian. There's a return to this authoritarian personality that people used to talk about in the 1950s. They want a strong leader, not someone who is thoughtful or introspective or is even thinking about democracy. I think democracy is in retreat.

Andrew Keen: I'd like you to try and separate the cause and effect of the information war. Are people longing for strong leaders because they're suffering from the vertigo of all this information, or are the propagandists in Moscow and Ankara and New Delhi and Manila and Budapest the ones manipulating the people?

Richard Stengel: I think democracies have done a poor job of educating people about what it means to be a citizen in a democracy. We've done a good job of educating people about the freedoms of democracy, the things they can do, but not the responsibilities. I remember Sandra Day O'Connor said to me, 'We're going to pay a terrible price in the US for having stopped teaching civics 40 years ago.' And we have paid that price.

You had people voting in America, and including the candidate running, who didn't know the three branches of government or what the responsibility of a citizen is in a democracy. And that primary responsibility is to be knowledgeable and to participate. I think we've taken agency away from people, and what people like about that is that it's a relief not to have to make a decision yourself. It's a relief not to have to learn about things and to listen to that strongman leader who is telling me what to believe.

Andrew Keen: We can't blame Facebook for that. We can't blame Putin for that. We can't even blame Donald Trump for that.

Richard Stengel: In fact, I actually think the opportunity for fixing democracy using those platforms and using technology is enormous. I think people overplay how they've undermined democracy and I think they underplay how much they can do to fix democracy. Why wouldn't Facebook be telling people here are the three branches of government? Here's your responsibility as a citizenship. That's non-partisan and that's bipartisan. The platforms can do that.

Andrew Keen: They can in a way, Rick, but you know better than anyone that the platforms aren't *Time* magazine. They don't create content. They are platforms that enable you and me to put photos of our babies on and our opinions. So how could these platforms transform themselves from echo chambers to serious publications that will inform a civic culture?

Richard Stengel: Well, remember, they started using third-party content and monetizing that, not creating content themselves but using pictures that we took of our kids or cats and we gave that to each other and then they sold advertising against it. Their whole model was different than the traditional press model, which was monetizing content that they'd created.

Are they publishers? Absolutely, but not in the traditional sense. One of the things that needs to change, at least in the US, is the perception of them according to the law as not being liable for their content.

Andrew Keen: The safe harbor…

Richard Stengel: Yes, and the fact that they're not liable for their content. In fact, the legislation was created with good intentions, which were that they didn't want the companies to censor people too much, but what they did was gave them a kind of immunity for all of this hate speech and negative content that they have. They need to be a little more responsible and they also need to become more like traditional publishers themselves and give people the kind of content to make them better citizens.

Andrew Keen: Rick, you know Silicon Valley pretty well. These guys don't really get it do they? I mean, if you said to Mark Zuckerberg, 'I want you to use Facebook to make people more responsible as citizens, to make them better informed,' of course he'd nod and smile and say, 'That's a great idea,' but he wouldn't really get it and he certainly wouldn't help you.

Richard Stengel: I disagree – I think he would get it. I think he comes from this earlier vision of the internet as the great democratization of information that actually gave people agency, not only to learn but to communicate. Every person was a journalist and so I think he gets that, and I think he is dismayed by what has happened and certainly by the impression that people have that the internet is undermining our democracy. I don't think he wants that and I don't think the other Silicon Valley companies want it either.

In fact, their whole business premise is about people being able to make decisions about the content they consume. In authoritarian states, people don't make that decision about the content they consume. In Russia, people can consume whatever they want but they only consume state information. That happens in all of these other countries, too – in China, in Turkey where there has been this strongman kind of politics.

Andrew Keen: But isn't there a problem with the Silicon Valley business model, certainly the business model of companies like Facebook and Google, where they give these platforms for free and then make money through advertising? Again it's a bit of a joke, but as Chief Marketing Officer of America you never collected up the data of all American citizens and sold them to advertisers, which is essentially what Facebook does.

Richard Stengel: Yes, but I also think that's where legislation has to change. The legislation has to err on the side of privacy, and what a lot of people don't realize is Americans have more privacy protections than Europeans and than people around the world do, from the government. What they don't have privacy protections from is Facebook and Google, that you give your most intimate information to. We need to be protected from them selling that information. We need to know when they're selling it and to whom they're selling it. There must be much more transparency and I think the platform companies realize that too and are getting ready for that day.

Andrew Keen: So let's focus more specifically on the fixes to democracy. Can the free market solve the core problems of democracy?

Richard Stengel: One of the core ideas of information in a democracy is this idea of the 'marketplace of ideas'. It comes from John Stuart Mill and Milton, and Justice Holmes wrote about it in a famous free speech case which was this idea that the truth will win out in the marketplace of ideas. It's a lovely thought; I've always believed it. But now the marketplace of ideas is changing and it's a different kind of market. That was a much more idealistic view, that somehow truth will win out over falsehood, but with the rise of disinformation, the truth doesn't win out in the marketplace of ideas. There's a wholly different market and so we have to think about it in a different way than we used to think about it in the twentieth century.

Andrew Keen: So you believe in this absolute idea of truth, that there could be a winning out?

Richard Stengel: I actually don't. What I believe in is media literacy. I used to say in government, 'We don't have a fake news problem, we have a media literacy problem.' People don't understand information and they don't understand the provenance of information; they don't understand how to tell the difference between something factual and not factual, and that's a problem. We need to teach that in schools. That needs to be taught like we teach mathematics and writing.

Andrew Keen: You think that could solve some of the problems with online propaganda and lies?

Richard Stengel: I think it would solve a lot. Lots of people, including Mark Zuckerberg, think that AI can solve 80 per cent of the problem. Let's just suggest that they're right about that, but individual knowledge of how to separate fact from fiction could do the last 20 per cent. In fact, one of the things I believe is that media entities, journalistic entities need to be much more transparent about what they do.

When you publish news online, you can publish the full text of the interview. You can publish all the research you do. That would help inform readers that a gigantic amount of work went into this. That the writer checked it. He had two or three sources for everything. She did all this research. Right now we present stories and don't see how they're prepared. I think people should see how they're prepared.

Andrew Keen: So that is a new role for newspapers – rather than platforms for information, they also become teachers.

Richard Stengel: I always thought in my role as a journalist that I was a teacher. I was educating people about something that was important, and their role is to even teach people how to think about things. So if you see how a story is constructed, it helps you understand the importance of that kind of journalism and why it's something to be trusted as opposed to something not to be trusted.

Andrew Keen: This is all very well, but just as the internet has triggered the rise of disinformation, it's also killed a lot of newspapers. *Time* is not what it was and the *New York Times* and *Wall Street Journal* are doing okay, but we've seen regional newspapers decimated. So realistically, is this going to happen?

Richard Stengel: I'm not a sentimentalist about this. When I think back, why did every newspaper in every American city in the twentieth century have a correspondent in Paris? Well because the story from Paris, if you're reading the *New York Times*, you couldn't read it in the *Philadelphia Inquirer*, you couldn't read it in the *Chicago Tribune*, you couldn't read it in the *LA Times*. There was no internet. There was no way of a consumer doing that.

Now, do you need it? Does every newspaper need a Paris correspondent? I can read French newspapers on my phone. I can read what the *New York Times* correspondent says. The technology made a lot of those newspapers necessary because people didn't have access to information. Now they have access to much more information, so of course there's a lot of disruption in the field, and there's much more access to information. I mean, a kid in Vanuatu can read the entire contents of the British Museum Library on his phone, and that's a remarkable thing in human history. That's a tremendous benefit and in some ways it outweighs the loss of certain publications.

Andrew Keen: One of the things I got from your book, Rick, is that as Chief Marketing Officer of the United States in the Obama Administration, you learned the power and the value of storytelling. To conclude, tell me a story about democracy. Tell me a story that's powerful.

Richard Stengel: One of the things that actually moved me when I was in government and is on the soft power end of things is that under me were all these educational exchanges. There are millions of foreign students who come and study in America, and what I found powerful about talking to these students is they would come to the US and we would open the curtain to America and it wasn't so much about, 'Hey, this is the greatest place on earth.' The students would talk to me and would say, 'Why are there so many beggars in the streets?' 'Why, when I went to high school, did the black students sit together and the Asian students sit together?' But they saw that we were also telling these stories about ourselves and that we were open to our flaws. That, to me, is one of the virtues of democracy and it was something that was very powerful. So even if people didn't necessarily identify with America, they saw there's another model to the way states can be, the way that you can expose your own flaws to your own citizens, and that only makes the loyalty of those citizens stronger. That was powerful to me.

CARL BENEDIKT FREY

I first met Carl Benedikt Frey at the top of a Bavarian mountain in August 2019. We were both participating in a DLD event that combined a conversation about the future with a vigorous hike. While I didn't know Carl personally, I was familiar with his academic work, and particularly with a much-cited 2013 Oxford University paper which warned that 47 per cent of current jobs are at risk from the digital revolution.

A few weeks later, I interviewed Carl about his important book, *The Technology Trap: Capital, Labor, and Power in the Age of Automation*. Like Paul-Bernhard Kallen, Carl uses the past – and particularly the history of nineteenth-century industrialization – to reinforce his belief in the digital twenty-first century. Yes, he acknowledges, 47 per cent of us might lose our current jobs because of automated technology, but the same thing happened in the nineteenth-century Industrial Revolution, and technology was subsequently able to create different kinds of jobs and a more prosperous society.

Andrew Keen: Carl Benedikt Frey, the Oxford Martin Citi Fellow and Co-Director of the Oxford Martin Programme on Technology and Employment at the Oxford Martin School; Carl, you're also the author of an extremely important new book *The Technology Trap: Capital, Labor, and Power in the Age of Automation*. Carl, to begin, what exactly is the technology trap?

Carl Frey: The technology trap refers to the period up until the first Industrial Revolution and the fact that during this period the politically powerful had little to gain and much to lose from the introduction of any technology that threatened their interests.

And as a result of this, economic growth was stagnant for a long time. So particularly the craft guilds would have nothing that replaced their skills, jobs, and income and as a result of that, the governments typically sided with the craft guilds, fearing political and social unrest.

Andrew Keen: Are you suggesting then that the dominant classes are essentially Luddites?

Carl Frey: Well, in a way they certainly were, I think for different reasons; the craftsmen were certainly Luddites and the people who smashed machinery during the Industrial Revolution in England, but Luddism was widespread. Luddism has become this popular expression referring to particular episodes, but workers smashing machines occurred in Germany, in France, and several occasions in China and India and so on. So this was the state of affairs up until the nineteenth century.

Andrew Keen: Why do you think the term Luddite has taken on such a pejorative meaning, given as you suggest that most people were against technological change in the nineteenth century and it might be said that the same is true today?

Carl Frey: I think it's because of the experience of the past 200 years. It's noteworthy, if we go back, that commentators of the time like Marx, Engels, Thomas Malthus, and David Ricardo all agreed that mechanization couldn't boost wages.

And the experience of the late nineteenth and twentieth century showed essentially that was wrong. As automation progressed, as people acquired new skills and shifted into new jobs, people became a lot better off, not just in terms of incomes but also in terms of the quality of working life in general. Not too long before, a lot of people worked in the coalmines where they wouldn't see daylight for weeks, cave-ins and explosions were part of everyday working life, and lung disease was part of their work package. And today most people in the industrial West work in air-conditioned offices, so working conditions have improved a lot as well.

I think a lot of people that look with a very dismissive view on the Luddites take this very long-term perspective, and what they miss is that the Luddites were essentially right because they were not the ones that benefited from technological change. Wages were stagnant or falling for seven decades, as the Industrial Revolution took off. Some of them with the benefit of hindsight could have taken some comfort that the next generations were better off as a result of this, but they had no way of knowing.

Andrew Keen: So let's fast-forward a couple of hundred years, because the point of your book is not the Industrial Revolution but today's digital revolution, and particularly the smart machine, the AI revolution of today. Do you think there are a lot of close analogies between the early part of the twenty-first century and the early parts of the nineteenth century?

Carl Frey: Yes, and that is the key theme of my book. That is not to suggest that everything in history repeats – there are many differences as well, but many of the economic trends are very similar.

During the nineteenth century we saw a hollowing out of middle-income jobs. We saw that wages fell behind output growth, which is a way of saying that labor share of income was falling. And we saw a lot of not just economic but also social and political polarization, quite similar to what we're seeing today.

The big difference, of course, is that the Luddites didn't have any political rights. Property ownership remained a requirement for voting throughout the nineteenth century, and as a result of that they voted with sticks and stones. Today people can show in general elections and what we've been seeing over the past four decades or so is that as economies have deindustrialized, a particular group of men with no more than a high school degree, who would have flocked into the factories before the age of automation, their wages have consistently fallen over this period of time.

So for all the talk of inequality, the real issue is that a significant group has been made worse off in the labor market as a result of technological change, just as the Luddites were. And they've also to some extent lost their political voice. If you go back to the 1950s and 1960s, you'll see that high-income voters tend to be associated with the political right and that low-education, low-income voters tend to be associated with the political left. And that changes from the 1970s and 1980s onwards, as the political left becomes increasingly associated with educated voters.

And so, in sum, what has happened is that this group has been left disenfranchised by the mainstream political parties and the populists are tapping into their anger very effectively.

Andrew Keen: Is the difference, or maybe it's a similarity, that it's not entirely clear what people are going to do in the AI revolution? I'm sure you will say that it wasn't entirely clear what people were going to do when they left the land at the beginning of the nineteenth century.

Carl Frey: I think that's absolutely right. And I think what people will do to some extent depends on what the technology does, and whether it replaces people's skills or augments them in a way that allows them better wages and increases their bargaining power.

But it is not entirely clear how this will play out, in terms of political responses. We struggle to predict the outcome of a general election even on the day it happens, so it's very hard to predict future political events. A key point of the book is that there have been a lot of studies that focus on long-term trends in technology and that try to predict what the labor market will look like in 30 years or so. And we put out a study a while ago estimating that 47 per cent of American jobs are at risk of being automated.

Andrew Keen: That's a study that I've quoted many times and I know for many other people it's become the most authoritative study warning about the implication on employment of the digital revolution.

Carl Frey: Just to clarify, what we say in this study is not that any of these jobs *will* be automated but what we're trying to say is how many jobs are potentially at risk from a technological capabilities point of view, so we're looking at the potential scope of automation.

And there are a lot of economic and social factors that will determine the pace of adoption. I think a mistake that a lot of people made is that social and political factors play a huge role. And if progress was inevitable the Industrial Revolution would have happened a bit earlier in the history of mankind. And if progress and the adoption of new technologies were inevitable, every country today would be rich.

So it's pretty clear from the historical record and from the current state of affairs that technological progress is not inevitable, and that is the key message of the book.

Andrew Keen: And of course it's a really important message that technological progress isn't inevitable just through technology, because of the complexity and somewhat arbitrary nature of political and social progress.

So standing back, of course we don't know everything about the future, but what should the government be doing in terms of regulating big tech, regulating AI, and steering it in a way that will benefit the population – the citizens rather than just small groups of technologists?

Carl Frey: I think we need to be very humble about our ability to direct technological change. Usually that hasn't worked from a top-down approach, in terms of steering in which direction innovation should go. And I think countries that are behind the frontiers of technology and that adopt technologies that have already been put in use elsewhere are to some extent able to do that by playing catch-up, but when we expand the frontiers of technology into the unknown, it's very hard to steer for them.

What we can do, though, is help people adjust to technological change, and I think there are certain patterns that tend to repeat themselves. The way that people have adjusted to technological change in the past is (a) by acquiring new skills, and (b) moving to where new jobs are emerging. And I think there's a tendency to focus on one big idea, like universal basic income, but in fact there are a lot of smaller things that can be seen as minor individually that make a big difference collectively.

Andrew Keen: So what are the new jobs of the future, Carl? In this age of automation, are they the low-pay, precariat jobs of Uber drivers and Airbnb renters, or are they going to be new categories of well-paid, high-skilled jobs in an age of the smart machine?

Carl Frey: I think both, but if we go back to the nineteenth century and I'd asked my great-grandmother what she thought the generation of her great-grandchildren were going to be working as, she wouldn't have said, 'Well, I think they're going to be software engineers or working on technology or as hot yoga instructors and travel agents and so on.'

And in a similar way, I think we're ill-placed to predict exactly what the jobs of the future will be, but I do think there are certain patterns. The machines still perform quite poorly when it comes to complex social interactions. They do okay in basic text communication, but even there they are not great, and they're nowhere near outperforming us in in-person social interactions.

And I think at the same time we'll see new technologies creating entirely new jobs in tech industries, like the jobs of big data architects, AI auditors, Android developers and so on. And what happens when a new tech job is created in a place like the Bay Area is that a person goes out and goes to the hairdresser, goes grocery shopping, takes a taxi and so on, and that creates on average five new jobs in the local service economy, and some of these will be new jobs, like Zumba instructors, which only appeared quite recently – we tend to care more about our fitness and health, the wealthier we get.

And the problem though is that it creates a lot of pressure on housing in those places because as economic activity becomes increasingly clustered, we need to build more in the places where new jobs are emerging, and that has failed to happen. As a result, the main beneficiaries of this have been owners of real estate in those places, and what's even worse is that has kept out a lot of people from where the growth is happening, which means that productivity growth has been slower than it otherwise would have been, which means that because people can't move into the productive sectors of the economy their wages are falling behind and it's leading to growing inequality as well. So a lot of it has to do with the geography of new jobs.

Andrew Keen: And on the political front, how should we be confronting nostalgic populism, this idea that yesterday was better and that we want to go back to the certainties of the past? How are we going to build political parties that embrace the future not just on the part of a tiny minority of technologists, but for everybody?

Carl Frey: Well, I think we need to combat it with nostalgic pragmatism – winning the argument and showing them that we have the solutions. And the solutions are very practical: you need to get rid of zoning restrictions in those locations to allow companies and public institutions to build more, to keep house prices down. And we need to do more in terms of investing in infrastructure to actually connect places.

So where I grew up in southern Sweden, for example, Malmo is a city that specialized in building ships and as the shipyard closed down the city was doing poorly for a long time. Up until the construction of the bridge to Copenhagen – which allowed the people to stay put in Malmo where mobile housing was cheap and commute to Copenhagen where there was an abundance of better-paying jobs – most of them would spend most of their earnings locally where they lived, which gave a boost to the local service economy there and created a virtuous cycle.

I think these are just a few of many seemingly relatively minor things that governments can do to help. And I think it's increasingly clear that the populists don't have the solutions, and I think the only way of dealing with their appeal over the medium term is to show that we have the solutions.

Andrew Keen: Do we need new political parties? You talked about a nostalgic pragmatism; are there new pragmatic politicians, parties, or ideologies that you think will be effective vehicles for driving us forward in the twenty-first century?

Carl Frey: I think here in the UK we do need new political parties and I'm hesitant to say 'we' because I'm actually Swedish but I have lived here for nearly ten years. And no, what we're seeing is that both Labour and the Conservatives are essentially split and a new political dividing line has become localist versus globalist, and that's tearing across parties.

So I do think that we need new parties and the political landscape is to some extent already being reshaped, but that's different from country to country.

Andrew Keen: You're not cheering me up, Carl. It doesn't seem as if we're responding very effectively. You're suggesting some solutions, some remedies, but there aren't any political movements. Populism is on the rise everywhere. People are nostalgic for an imaginary past. Technologists are increasingly unpopular, particularly in Silicon Valley. We have this aggregation of monopolistic power, in technological terms. Is it possible that this is all going to end very badly, in social cultural revolution, in bloodshed on the streets?

Carl Frey: It would be foolish to exclude the possibility but let's go back to the Luddites. At the time, ordinary people didn't have a political voice. There was no educational system to help people adjust. This logic persisted, so most people believed that income growth in per capita terms wasn't even possible, and so as a result of that there was no need for a welfare system to help people that struggled to adjust. And 200 years later puts the concerns of that time in perspective.

I think perspective is what you need and if we go back historically we'll see we've been through many of these debates before and I think if you lived in this period, it was very hard to see a way out because you were stuck in the echo chamber of the time you lived in.

And I think what history shows us is that we're actually quite good at coming up with solutions, and technological progress can be enormously disruptive in the short term and there's no guarantee that we'll deal with it effectively. But at least the historical record should provide us with some hope.

Andrew Keen: It does, but doesn't it provide us with the lesson that regulation and the role of the state is essential? You poo-pooed that a little bit earlier in our conversation, but doesn't the history of the Industrial Revolution, with the creation of social safety nets and changes in the law when it comes to unionization, the organization of labor and the many other institutional reforms that went with the Industrial Revolution, point to the fact that the only real change is going to happen through the state and through regulation?

Carl Frey: I think that's broadly right. If we look historically, it's clear that the regulation has played a role. When the automobile was invented, they didn't have traffic laws. It's true that governments pushed for electrification and making that technology available to everyone. It's also true that Labour fought for democracy, but that was more of a bottom-up movement that started to demand democratic rights rather than governments doing it from the top down.

And so I think it's a matter of clearly adjusting our institutions, investing in education, doing a lot of things that we've done in the past. When we speak about regulation though it depends on what the regulation is because the people writing the regulations tend to be the interest groups of today, and those interest groups may not write regulations in a way that benefits future business and start-ups, and so on.

So I think that there is a tendency to over-emphasize regulation, and we need to focus more on helping people adjust and on making sure that the bits of the welfare state that work well continue to work well, and build upon that.

TOOMAS ILVES

My first meeting with Toomas Ilves was in the formal dining room of the baroque eighteenth-century presidential palace in Tallinn in Estonia. That was in 2016 and Ilves was still president of Estonia, a position he'd held since 2006. As the pioneer of Estonian digital democracy, President Ilves spoke passionately about his e-democratic experiment to rebuild trust in government and establish a more transparent bureaucracy. He also argued that the establishment of a viable digital democracy required the rethinking of our right to privacy. In the digital twenty-first century, President Ilves believed, we need to trade our right to anonymity for guarantees that nobody will be able to look at our personal data without our permission.

Our second meeting occurred in much less auspicious circumstances. In late 2019, I met Ilves at his small ground-floor office in Stanford University. The subject of our conversation was similar to the one three years earlier: fixing democracy, he continues to believe, requires not only embracing digital technology but also rethinking twentieth-century assumptions about individual privacy and anonymity. His country's e-democratic experiment, the former president argues, offers a way to rebuild trust not only in government but also in experts. And it's also the best antidote to the authoritarian populism being peddled by the 'yesterdays' running Russia, Estonia's eastern neighbor.

Andrew Keen: Toomas Ilves, as president of Estonia you pioneered a very innovative kind of electronic democracy, particularly bound up with the internet. How much of your thinking about the Estonian e-democratic experiment was triggered by the experience of being so close to Russia and of being subjected to the so-called 'first digital world war' in 2007?

Toomas Ilves: Well, we were so far along our path in 2007 that we'd already made our decisions, our policies had been worked out, and we had implemented all kinds of innovative solutions. Rather, I would say that the reason Estonia chose this path was that we saw this as a way to leapfrog in development, because when we became independent in 1991 we were so far behind.

And so we saw technology as a way to leapfrog a lot of development, to be on a level playing field with other countries because while the other advanced rich countries had had 50 years to build great roads and new hospitals, all the physical infrastructure, the digital infrastructure was so primitive everywhere that my argument to the government at the time was that this is the way we can catch up because this is a place where we're not behind.

Andrew Keen: It wasn't just about catching up; wasn't it also about deepening democracy and improving democracy?

Toomas Ilves: Well, it was fundamentally a way of getting society to work on a new basis in a way that there was greater participation.

Andrew Keen: Citizenship?

Toomas Ilves: Citizenship or inclusivity. Also very important for us was to reduce a rural-urban divide in development; people feeling that they don't have to be in the capital city to be doing all kinds of things that you want to do. It was seen as a new way – and still is – of organizing society to increase participation.

Andrew Keen: Do you think that one of the problems with contemporary democracy is that there's too much noise – that we need more silence, we need to be able to listen?

Toomas Ilves: Well, the decibel level that you will find on social media is absurdly high. You may be sitting silently but what you basically have is people screaming.

Andrew Keen: Even in Estonia, where people don't tend to scream too much?

Toomas Ilves: Well, there's a silent scream there as well.

Andrew Keen: A Munchian scream.

Toomas Ilves: Well, I think it's quite apt. While the political situation in Estonia has changed very recently, I would argue that the decibel level and the brutishness of discourse that we did not have in Estonia before is something that we have acquired from being on social media, which in general has a level of discourse that you would not have before a widespread digital society, all over the world.

Andrew Keen: When you see the crisis of democracy all over the world, from the United States to Britain, to Italy, to Hungary, to Poland, what do you think they can most learn from your e-democratic experience? Why should they come to Estonia and look at what you've done?

Toomas Ilves: Well, for one, I think that the amount of frustration that you run into simply living your life as a citizen is greatly reduced by having the efficiencies. But I am sitting in Stanford and in a 12-mile radius are the headquarters of Tesla, Apple, Google, Facebook, Palantir, and who knows how many others bubbling under the billion-dollar companies, and it's amazing what this place has produced. On the other hand, you try to interact here with any public service, with the government, with any agency, the school district, anything in the public sector is in the 1950s or at best the 1960s – all paper-based, standing in line, taking a number, bureaucracy that takes forever.

Andrew Keen: If the DMV experience magnifies…

Toomas Ilves: The DMV is probably the best example, but it is in everything.

Andrew Keen: And do you think that digitalizing those services makes us better citizens? Do you have evidence from Estonia of that?

Toomas Ilves: Um, well no academic studies, but—

Andrew Keen: But anecdotal, or your experience? I mean, you pioneered this thing...

Toomas Ilves: Well certainly, when you have far more efficient services you don't stand in line at DMV for hours and hours, and I think you have happier citizens, frankly.

Andrew Keen: And better citizens, happier, more responsible?

Toomas Ilves: Well, I think if you're happy, you're less likely to go and leave in a huff and drive your car into someone.

Andrew Keen: Trust levels in Estonia about government are much higher than they are certainly in the United States or Western Europe?

Toomas Ilves: It's interesting, because at the political level here it's like, 'The guys in government they're all awful, stupid, corrupt,' and I think you find that in all democracies. But there's a difference in the government side, which is that the administration, the way you do interact with the government, is you trust the system. Since we instituted the system we have, it has not failed. No leaks, no damage, and so you get used to the efficiencies. You get used to things working, as opposed to standing in line.

Andrew Keen: So your argument then is that your digital reforms have strengthened democracy, whether it's electronic or analog in Estonia?

Toomas Ilves: I would say that people trust governance more here. Much of it actually has to do with corruption reduction. Estonia is by far the least corrupt post-communist country, but in the European Union we are in the upper part of the EU in terms of having low corruption. And through digitization you eliminate all kinds of opportunities for corruption which you see rampant around the world, not at the high level but rather at the lower level, where in so much of the world in order to get a basic service you have to pay some money to your local official for something.

I remember talking about this in Greece, and they said, 'We call it speed-up cash.' And it's an interesting dichotomy that the high-level corruption that makes the headlines is someone paying someone in the government to do something illegal. The problem in most of the world for the average citizen is that you have to pay a government official to do what he's supposed to do.

So here you get this boost in trust and governance, thanks to the fact that you've eliminated the opportunity to demand someone to pay something, to fill out a form, to register something; it's all digital. So say you want to apply for a child benefit, you don't have to go there and stand in line and fill out a form and then have someone say, 'Give me some money.' We know that you live there and we know from your taxes that you have three kids and therefore this entitles you to this. Or we know you've reached this age and that you now are a senior citizen and you get a discount on movie theaters or the bus.

Andrew Keen: Is the electronic democratic experiment in Estonia re-architecting the basic social contract between citizen and government, when it comes to accountability and anonymity?

Toomas Ilves: Accountability so often has to do with a low-level civil servant who will not do his job, whereas if you eliminate that part of the citizen-governance interaction you just tick off the boxes, basically. That's what it comes down to – you tick off the boxes. You're entitled to this; you're not entitled to that. That issue of is the government accountable or not doesn't come up.

On the anonymity side, well that is I think more of a problem of the non-governmental sphere – people look at the Estonia thing and say, 'What about privacy?' And I would say I'm much more worried about privacy in a paper world than I am about privacy in a digital world because in the system that we have, we know that anyone who has access to your data, there's a log file on that interaction.

In my country, when I was in office, my property is all listed there, so anyone can go and look at what property I have. And the other side is that I get to see who is looking at it, so the yellow press would regularly check, 'Oh, has he bought anything?'

Andrew Keen: So doing away with anonymity gives citizens more power?

Toomas Ilves: Well, in the sense that you can't go sneaking in there. Now there are much bigger cases with medical records, when the racing car driver Michael Schumacher had this horrible accident a couple of years ago, within hours the largest newspapers in Europe had pictures of his X-rays. That could not happen in my country, only a doctor who is actually authorized to look at his records would see it, and we would know that this person went and accessed these data at that time.

So it doesn't happen, so in a paper world you just go into a filing cabinet and pull out the thing and make a photocopy, put it back in and no one knows. So the accountability is much greater there.

Where I see the problem is that the public sphere has become in the internet era so nasty, and there are all kinds of things there – doxing, for example. When the woman who during the Kavanaugh hearings here testified against him, she had a huge number of death threats and last I heard, which is about three months ago, she had been forced to move four times from where she lived because anonymously someone would publish where she lived.

Andrew Keen: So anonymity is a threat to democracy?

Toomas Ilves: I would argue that yes, it is.

Andrew Keen: Plus, you have, of course, the disinformation campaigns being orchestrated by anonymous people who perhaps are working in St. Petersburg or Moscow or Beijing or somewhere...

Toomas Ilves: One of the problems we face in a digital era is that you don't know who is doing what. And this was summed up in this 1993 *New Yorker* cartoon of two dogs, and one dog says to the other, 'On the internet no one knows you're a dog.' And there are no social constraints on behavior, so you can say the nastiest stuff and you can do the nastiest stuff, without any fear of any kind of accountability.

And that absence of accountability, I think, is extremely dangerous, has been extremely dangerous, and will continue to be.

Andrew Keen: And the e-democracy experiment in Estonia does undermine anonymity. It may not do away with it entirely, but it certainly challenges this in some way.

Toomas Ilves: Well, in the governance domain we still don't know. The media is full of anonymous stories and commentaries and so forth, but at least pulling out someone's healthcare record – you can't do that.

Andrew Keen: Do you think in the long run, the only way to protect truth and democracy is by somehow fixing this problem of anonymity?

Toomas Ilves: Oh absolutely. I think, however, there are certain caveats. One of them is that liberal democracies need to do that. As soon as you say that anonymity is bad, you'll say, 'Well, what about the dissidence in some authoritarian country? And what about them?' Well, for ourselves in our democratic space where we respect human rights and so forth, that is not a problem.

I admit that if you're living in North Korea, if you were to have access to the internet there, you might want to have anonymity. But on the other hand, I would also argue that in those authoritarian countries it does not exist anyway, because they know who you are. China is probably the best example.

Andrew Keen: But in the West, in Western democracies, is the only way to fix the wars of misinformation and disinformation and the undermining of truth, to confront this issue of anonymity?

Toomas Ilves: I think we have no choice. I'm not sure it will happen yet but…

Andrew Keen: It's not going to be popular.

Toomas Ilves: It'll be extremely unpopular. On the other hand, if you look at the damage done to people through anonymity, then I think we have an obligation as democracies to defend people's rights, and again if someone is going to start publishing, 'Oh, he lives there or she lives there', and then you get death threats or even worse, you have this phenomenon here in the United States where an anonymous phone call will come in and say, 'In this house there's this horrible crime going on there.' And of course SWAT teams go out and break in the door and it turns out there's nothing there and sometimes people have been shot because of trigger-happy SWAT team members. Or someone gets a heart attack because they're shocked when these ten guys run in with masks and helmets and bulletproof vests.

So those are clear dangers to the well-being of citizens that I think will after some horrible case ultimately lead to some kind of legislation.

Andrew Keen: Finally, what haven't you achieved on the e-democracy front in Estonia that you think you need to achieve to make it a genuine electronic democracy?

Toomas Ilves: What I really see is that I think that there's not much more we can do in the current context. What really needs to be done in a Europe where people travel all the time, go to different places, is that we really need to make the same kind of service we have in Estonia so that we have digital prescriptions. I mean, if I get sick I can write to my doctor and I can go to any pharmacy and get a prescription.

But if I go to even Latvia, the next-door neighbor, I can't do that; I've actually run into that problem when I went to France, where I came down with a horrible flu when I was supposed to speak in front of a full session of the European Parliament; otherwise I could have called my doctor and said, 'Well, send me this prescription and I can go to a pharmacy.'

Or even more, say I want to go to Greece and something happens to me and I go to a doctor. The doctor probably knows English but he certainly isn't going to know Estonian, so I would just authorize my doctor to see my medical records and he would see them translated into Greek so he could say, 'Oh, you're allergic to this and you had that operation' and whatever.

Those are elementary services for us; they are unbelievable services for the rest of Europe and I believe that if we were to move Europe in that direction, you'd have a lot less of the kind of anti-European feeling that we have.

The other thing I would say is that basically what you can see happening are three different models of how to approach this digital world. We have the US laissez-faire capitalist model, which basically says, 'Let's monetize any information, everyone's data, and we'll make a lot of money and be very rich.'

There's the Chinese model, which is, 'Let's surveil everyone and monetize everything, but also information will go to the government.' And then there's a third slower approach on the part of Europe, which has so far been much more humane and privacy-centered, that says, 'Let's look at what is legitimate for governments to do and what is legitimate for companies to do. Where do we have this clash between privacy, freedom of speech?' They're wrestling with it but I think that in Europe we are coming up with a better way of doing things than this kind of rampaging through everyone's data.

Andrew Keen: And the third model of those three models from the point of view of democracy, the best one is Europe?

Toomas Ilves: If I project into the future, yes. I think it is, because I do not trust the absence of genuine privacy and personal data security in the United States. We see every other day another 100 million persons' data are stolen, with limited recourse, that the citizenry becomes potential victims of people who want to do harm.

From that point of view, I think having severe restrictions on private data, personal data being used and sold and commodified is something that will become more and more of an issue in liberal democracies that value human rights. You already see the European privacy legislation, GDPR, being adopted by the state of California. They just took it and tweaked it a little bit but it applies here.

I think that there will be a groundswell of antagonism toward the mass sale of every citizen's data that we see right now.

SCOTT GALLOWAY

There are few better public speakers than Scott Galloway, and his annual performance at the DLD conference in Munich is always a highlight. In front of a crowd of several hundred people, he prowls the stage, ridiculing Facebook's promise to make the world a better place, exposing the economic power of Amazon, and confirming the creepy informational ubiquity of Google. Not only does he seem to singlehandedly take on what he dubs the 'Big Four' of Apple, Google, Amazon, and Facebook but he beats them with his corrosive wit and his mastery of the nuances of the digital economy.

So how effective are his oratorical skills in the more intimate medium of a podcast interview? He is convincing in his arguments in favor of breaking up Google, Amazon, and Facebook (but not Apple, interestingly), in order to protect the start-up entrepreneurs of the innovation economy against these trillion-dollar digital leviathans. It may even be the most effective strategy for controlling surveillance capitalism. Like so many other thinkers in this anthology, Scott looks to history to build his case for fixing the future. Anti-trust was essential for smashing the cartels of the industrial age, he reminds us, and it's essential today if we are to build a more efficient and fairer economy.

Andrew Keen: Scott Galloway, the author of *The Fall*, a book about the winner-take-all nature of the digital economy. Scott, the internet promised the democratization of business and culture. The reverse seems to have been the case. What's gone wrong?

Scott Galloway: Wow; we're going to need a longer show.

Andrew Keen: Easy question to begin, right?

Scott Galloway: Yeah, I think that these are for-profit entities and what they have kind of stumbled onto I would say, and there's a variety of things, but if you were to try and reverse engineer to one thing that's done a ton of damage it's that their underlying business models tap into a very tribal instinct, and that is we're very drawn to conflict and rage, and the underlying business model of Google and Facebook is to sell as much advertising as possible. So as a result, the algorithm has a vested interest in creating conflict and rage. So they talk about engagement as a key metric and what they really refer to is 'enragement'.

So, if someone posts a message talking about the science around the utility of vaccines it doesn't get much attention, but if someone posts something on the anti-vax movement and inspires a huge argument online, that's more Nissan ads. So there's an underlying motivation to tear at the fabric and separate us and create conflict, such that you end up with organizations that are very remiss to remove hate content and so they kind of set up a town square where people are shoved against each other and promoted to fight with one another. We have a business model that is meant to agitate and tear at the fabric of society.

Andrew Keen: Do the Americans then need to take a lead from the Europeans and focus on anti-trust, and aggressively fight the power and influence of these companies?

Scott Galloway: I think so. I think that what you're seeing from Europe is that they register all of the downsides of big tech – the job destruction, the tax avoidance, the weaponization of these platforms to pervert our elections – but they receive a fraction of the upside. In the US, they inspire a lot of innovation, a lot of revenue, a lot of jobs, but in Europe there are very few hospital wings or universities named after Google or Facebook billionaires. So while you capture all of the downside of big tech, you capture a fraction of the upside which stiffens the backbone of EU regulators, specifically Margrethe Vestager, and we're seeing not anti-trust as much because it's difficult to break up a company that's headquartered in another country, but we've seen more regulation and what I would call a more sober discussion around the downside of big tech in Europe.

Andrew Keen: What specifically would you like to see happen in the US, when it comes to controlling and harnessing the power of these huge tech companies?

Scott Galloway: I think we have a tendency in the US to either see things as good or bad, and if we see it as good, we leave it alone. I think pesticides are probably a net good for society, but we have a Food and Drug Administration. I think fossil fuels are still a net good for society, but we have emissions standards and we're investing aggressively in alternate forms of energy. I think big tech is on the whole a net good for society, but it's the word 'net' that is the problem. And I think that these companies would be better for their shareholders, broader tax base, more hiring, and more competitive – I think competition is the answer and I think anti-trust, breaking Google up into several companies as well as Facebook, would create entities that have to offer their customers, which are their advertisers, stronger value proposition.

So we would have to say to an advertiser, we're going to make the requisite investments to ensure that this platform is never weaponized by the foreign intelligence arm of the Russian government, or a competitor to YouTube might decide to create a genuinely safe place for kids on their platform. Right now there's very little incentive for them to do anything that gets in the way of their supernova business model of profitability, so it's a lot of faux concern, it's a lot of promises to do better, it's incredibly deft delay and obfuscation but monopoly behavior is a function of they don't really need to do anything. So in sum, I think a really good start would be to break these companies up.

Andrew Keen: Break them up? The Silicon Valley giants?

Scott Galloway: Yes, I think breaking them up would actually result in stronger companies. AT&T was considered an innovator in the 1970s and 1980s. You could call from New Jersey to California for 20 or 30 cents a minute, which seemed like a great deal at the time. And what we found when we broke them up into, I believe it was seven or nine Baby Bells, was that a lot of technology was lying dormant in their R&D lab Bell Labs. And we ended up unleashing a torrent of innovation, whether it was cell or fiber or data and analytics.

So we don't know what we're missing, in the sense that I believe that if you broke these companies up, you'd end up with companies that in aggregate are actually worth more. I think it would benefit shareholders, competition would be a wonderful thing to introduce into this ecosystem per our previous comments, broader tax base, more hiring, more mergers and acquisitions.

Andrew Keen: If you look at Google though, if you broke up Google, where's the value of the company outside YouTube and the Google search engine?

Scott Galloway: Well, I think that would be a great place to start and I think within 30 days of the break-up, if Google launches a video platform and YouTube launches a search engine, overnight we'd have two viable competitors instead of one in each category, because right now they're coordinating and cooperating. And as a result YouTube really doesn't have that much incentive to figure out a way not to radicalize our youth.

But if there were two of them, I think one of them would raise their hand and go we're going to make the requisite investment to have a stronger value proposition to stakeholders, to regulators, and to our customers.

I also think there's probably an opportunity to decouple the backend. With the acquisition of DoubleClick they have a huge backend infrastructure around serving ads and online ads. There's all kinds of things. You could break up Android, but I think Google, a spin of YouTube would probably be a good place to start and my prediction is that a year after the spin, the two companies would be worth more in aggregate than the company is worth now.

Andrew Keen: If Facebook was broken up, do you think that the social network could survive as a stand-alone business without Instagram and its other products?

Scott Galloway: Yeah. Facebook is not growing as fast as the others, but Facebook I think has 2.7 billion people on their various platforms. Facebook is still the largest social network in the world, still an incredible engine and in addition Instagram as an independent company might be worth as much as Facebook right now. It's growing fast and it's doing really well. It hasn't been weaponized by bad actors. It's got a kind of cleaner feel to it. And WhatsApp is arguably the largest telco company in the world right now.

Andrew Keen: You've spoken and written a lot about Amazon as the biggest of the big four in many ways and perhaps the most threatening of these companies in the long run. I assume that if you broke Amazon up, you would split it into an e-commerce company and a web services company?

Scott Galloway: I think that's right. My prediction is by 2025 that Amazon Web Services will be the most valuable company in the world. Right now there's no pure play way for investors to play the Cloud. If you want to play Google Cloud you've got to crawl over a search engine. Azure, Microsoft's offering, you've got to crawl over Microsoft Office. Investors love pure plays because CEOs love diversified companies because it smooths out their earnings, but investors don't need CEOs to diversify for them, so they love pure play offerings and I think AWS on its own, being the number one in the fastest-growing, most profitable sector of technology the Cloud, would in three to five years be the most valuable company in the world.

So AWS, as a spin, I think helps shareholders and is better for the economy; I also think Amazon Fulfilment, the backend offering, could be a viable distinct competitor to FedEx and

UPS, and again wouldn't give them this unassailable advantage such that no e-commerce company could really make a dent in Amazon.

Also, I think you'd see a lot of e-commerce companies start to get funding, because right now no VC wants to fund any company that competes with Amazon. If you look at seed funding, the sectors that have had the biggest drop-off in seed funding are the sectors that compete with one of these four behemoths.

So these companies like to foment the false notion that we're living in an era of innovation, and if you read the *Wall Street Journal* and the *FT* and watch CNBC they propagate that false narrative. The reality is there were more new businesses being formed 40 years ago than there are now. There were twice as many companies being formed in the Carter Administration than there are now, because it is very difficult to start a company in the fastest growing parts of our economy because they're pretty much dominated by one or two companies in each of those sectors.

Andrew Keen: When it comes to Apple, the final of the big four, would you split that into a software and a hardware company, a device company and an entertainment company?

Scott Galloway: I think that's harder to do and because I think elegant anti-trust not only creates more competition but in the medium and long term benefits the shareholders of the original company. And I think it would be difficult to break Apple up because if you break up YouTube and Google, they're both great brands. You break up Facebook, Instagram, and WhatsApp – all three of them are great brands and do fine.

If you break up Apple, the difficult part is who gets the domain over the key asset which is the brand? So I don't see an elegant way to divide those two – I think in the case of Apple it's regulation of the App Store because a company like Spotify, a European company which in my view has a vastly superior offering, is growing more slowly than Apple Music because Apple is preinstalled on a billion devices, and when you searched for music in the App Store five years ago the number one return was Spotify. Now Spotify isn't in the top five – it's all Apple Music apps.

Andrew Keen: What is your historical take on the AI revolution? Is it something profoundly new, or is it really just more of the same?

Scott Galloway: I really don't have a lot of expertise around AI. It feels to me, as someone who watches technology and trends, like it's in a pretty serious hype cycle right now, along with virtual reality, the internet of things, 3D-printing. AI to me seems to take processing power to the next level and in terms of my life, the way AI impacts my life, is that if I'm watching *House of Cards*, season three, episode four, Netflix figures out that I might like season three, episode five, and begins playing it without me actually clicking on it.

But we'll see. It's being pitted as a nationalist argument that China, with its AI weaponized warriors, is coming for US AI firms. So I agree it's an exciting field, but I wonder if it's in a bit of a hype cycle right now where the dream and the fears of AI might not pay off or be realized as soon as people think.

Andrew Keen: Are the current incumbents, the big four, well set up to dominate AI, or will we have a Google or a Microsoft or an Apple of AI, a company that redefines the category?

Scott Galloway: I don't know. I think right now you'd have to say these companies are exceptionally well positioned, as are some Chinese companies – there appears to be a lot of funding and focused investment in China. But if you were to pick, these companies right now soak up the majority of the best human capital in the world. Amazon is the number one recruit out of my class. It used to be Goldman and it used to be American Express, and now it's Amazon.

Andrew Keen: Scott, you make a lot of sense at least in my mind on the breaking up of these big companies. Why aren't you in charge? You have a big platform, so why are these morons in

Washington, DC, still running the show – or perhaps more accurately *not* running the show? What's the problem here?

Scott Galloway: I've actually spent more time in Washington in the last six months than I've spent in the previous 20 years, and I have found the people in Washington to be pretty thoughtful and trying to address the problem. I find some of the work that our European regulators are doing in Brussels is actually quite thoughtful. Government is not known for moving crisply, but I do think the arc is slow but it bends toward justice in government. I do think they are starting to see the light around this.

And in the US what we're seeing is similar to tobacco. When states don't see their federal government moving as quickly as they'd like, that void gets filled by states. We have 48 attorney generals, with the exception of California and Puerto Rico, who have all signed on to investigate anti-trust concerns around Google and Facebook. So it's happening; we're heading in the right direction, but it's just maybe not heading as quickly as possible. And I love being an outsider – it frees you up to speak your mind. Being an academic is wonderful, getting to teach, so I'm in a great seat right now. And quite frankly, it's much easier to comment on things than it is to actually effect change, so I don't envy what our elected officials are facing every day.

Andrew Keen: Do you think if Elizabeth Warren is elected, and it certainly looks as if she's now the favorite to win the democratic nomination, that she will pursue a lot of the stuff that you're talking about, breaking up these big companies?

Scott Galloway: I do, but I think it's going to happen regardless. There might be certain individuals who move faster than others and she, to her credit, has been the most thoughtful and the most detailed and has obviously done the most homework. But this is a bipartisan issue. I wrote an article on the topic in *Esquire* magazine, and the first two calls I received after it was published were from legislative aides in Elizabeth Warren's office and also from Ted Cruz's office, who's a very conservative senator.

So the break-up of big tech, or concerns around the dangers of big tech, appears to be a rare bipartisan issue here in the US. Now there's some big obstacles: Amazon has 88 full-time lobbyists in DC. I think they're outgunned. There's so many distractions right now with our current Administration, that instead of focusing on various dumpster or forest fires, we're focused on different mushroom clouds of our own making by this Administration. So we're distracted from some key problems.

But I think there are reasons to be optimistic. I think Europe is making strides in looking at these problems. I think the states in the United States are looking at these problems. And I think whoever gets elected in 2020, maybe with the exception of Trump – I don't think he understands these issues and nor has he shown any competence to address them – but I think any Democrat that's elected, or maybe possibly any other Republican that's elected, is going to move against this issue.

Andrew Keen: Why isn't Silicon Valley more aggressively supportive of your position? After all, for most venture capitalists and entrepreneurs, it's in their interests to break these companies up and create a more competitive digital environment.

Scott Galloway: Well, a lot of them work for these companies, and a lot of them are in this ecosystem that benefits. If you think about these four companies, one way to look at them is as the most efficient vessels for the transfer of wealth from the rest of the world to the US, and then from the middle of the US to the coasts. So I'm not sure the Bay Area is in a hurry to turn on the lights at this cocaine-fueled party that's gone on to 6:00 a.m. and just see how ugly things are.

When it's raining money, it blurs your vision. Tobacco companies never made the connection between tobacco and cancer. Gun manufacturers will never make the connection between the sale of assault weapons and the murder of children. And I just don't think you're going to see the Bay Area-based tech ecosystem see the connection between the unfettered march of technology and what I believe is a key step to tyranny, and that is when government becomes co-opted by private power instead of being a countervailing force to it. And it feels as if we're getting dangerously close to that point.

Andrew Keen: Do you think there's something existential about the threat of big tech?

Scott Galloway: I think it's a big threat. If you look at what happened in Germany, what happened in Rwanda, typically an entity gets control of the media, gets control of the money, and it gets control of the military. And there's a direct correlation between the rise of these platforms in things ranging from white nationalism to the demonization of immigrants to teen depression, and so even if they have good intentions, the notion that any one company, if it were to be co-opted, weaponized or just come off the tracks, that we don't have countervailing forces in the form of competitors or a government that understands these platforms and is willing to push back on them, it puts us in a very dangerous place that history has shown does not end well.

Andrew Keen: So we really need to get our internet back?

Scott Galloway: That's right – let's take it back.

Andrew Keen: Well, you're the professor. Can't you educate these people to be more responsible?

Scott Galloway: Well, that's why I'm here now. That's why I'm talking with you.

The Interviewees

John Borthwick has been a leader and early stage investor in New York technology for over two decades. He is the founder and CEO of Betaworks, a start-up platform that builds and invests in companies across the social, data-driven media internet. Companies built by Betaworks include Giphy, Dots, bitly, TweetDeck, and Chartbeat. Early investments include Tumblr, Kickstarter, Medium, and Gimlet.

Ian Bremmer is a political scientist who helps business leaders, policy makers, and the general public make sense of the world around them. He is president of the Eurasia Group and GZERO Media. He has written ten books including, most recently, the *New York Times* bestseller *Us vs Them: The Failure of Globalism*.

Kenneth Cukier is senior editor at *The Economist* and the host of its weekly podcast on technology, *Babbage*. He is the co-author of the *New York Times* bestseller *Big Data*, which was translated into over 20 languages. Kenn is a board director of Chatham

House (the Royal Institute of International Affairs), a member of the Council on Foreign Relations, and an Associate Fellow at the University of Oxford's Saïd Business School.

Catherine Fieschi is the director of the new Global Policy Institute at Queen Mary University of London, as well as director of the London-based research group Counterpoint. Her research focuses on populist movements and forms of contemporary mobilization in Europe and across developed economies. She is the author of *Populocracy: The Tyranny of Authenticity and the Rise of European Populism.*

Rana Foroohar is the New York-based global business columnist and associate editor at the *Financial Times.* She is also CNN's global economic analyst. Her book, *Makers and Takers*, was shortlisted for the *Financial Times* McKinsey Book of the Year Award in 2016. Her latest book, *Don't Be Evil: How Big Tech Betrayed Its Founding Principles – and All of Us,* was published in November 2019.

Carl Benedikt Frey is a Swedish-German economist and economic historian. He is Oxford Martin Citi Fellow at Oxford University where he directs the programme on the Future of Work at the Oxford Martin School. He is author of *The Technology Trap: Capital, Labor, and Power in the Age of Automation.* Frey is also an Economics Associate of Nuffield

College and Senior Fellow at the Institute for New Economic Thinking, both at the University of Oxford.

Scott Galloway is a professor at New York University's Stern School of Business, where he teaches brand strategy and digital marketing. A serial entrepreneur, he has founded nine firms, including L2, Red Envelope, and Prophet. In 2012, he was named one of the World's 50 Best Business School Professors by Poets & Quants. His weekly YouTube series, *Winners and Losers,* has generated tens of millions of views.

Toomas Ilves is the former two-term president and foreign minister of Estonia who led his country's digitization since the beginning of the 1990s. He is currently a Distinguished Visiting Fellow at Stanford University.

David Kirkpatrick is a journalist and conference organizer. He spent 25 years at *Fortune* and created the BrainStorm Conference there, before leaving in 2008 to write *The Facebook Effect,* which was published in 2010. In 2011 he launched the Techonomy conference series and media company.

Eli Pariser is an author, activist, and entrepreneur focused on how to make technology and media serve democracy. In 2004, at the age of 23, he became executive director of MoveOn. org, where he helped pioneer the practice of online citizen engagement. His bestselling 2011 book, *The Filter Bubble,* introduced the term to the lexicon. He is currently Omidyar Fellow at the New America Foundation and co-directs the Civic Signals project at the National Conference on Citizenship.

Peter Pomerantsev is a Visiting Senior Fellow at the Institute of Global Affairs at the London School of Economics, an author, and a TV producer. His first book, *Nothing is True and Everything is Possible*, won the 2016 Royal Society of Literature Ondaatje Prize, and was nominated for the Samuel Johnson, *Guardian* First Book, Pushkin House, and Gordon Burns prizes. His most recent book is *This Is Not Propaganda: Adventures in the War Against Reality* (2019).

Maria Ressa is co-founder and CEO of the Philippines news resource Rappler.com. She was named 2018 *Time* magazine's Person of the Year for her work in protecting press freedom. She has also won the Golden Pen of Freedom Award from the World Association of Newspapers and News Publishers, the Knight International Journalism Award of the International Center for Journalists, the Gwen Ifill Press Freedom Award of the Committee to Protect Journalists and many other awards.

Douglas Rushkoff is a media theorist and activist who studies human autonomy in a digital age. His twenty books include *Team Human, Throwing Rocks at the Google Bus, Present Shock,* and *Program or Be Programmed.* He teaches at CUNY/Queens

College, hosts the *Team Human* podcast, and lectures around the world about humans, technology, and change.

Richard Stengel is the longest-serving Under Secretary of State for Public Diplomacy and Public Affairs in American history (2013–16). Before coming to the State Department, Stengel was the editor of *Time* for seven years. His latest book, *Information Wars: How We Lost the Global Battle Against Disinformation and What We Can Do About It*, was published in October 2019.

Peter Sunde is a Finnish-Norwegian artist and activist. He is co-founder of The Pirate Bay and the founder of Flattr. He is a socialist, a vegetarian, and is known in France as '*Le troll rêveur*'.

Ece Temelkuran is an award-winning Turkish writer and political commentator and the author of *How to Lose a Country: The Seven Steps from Democracy to Dictatorship*. She won the Edinburgh International Book Festival First Book award for her novel *Women Who Blow on Knots*, has been twice recognized as Turkey's most-read political columnist, and twice rated one of the ten most influential people in social media.

Martin Wolf is chief economics commentator at the *Financial Times*. He was awarded the CBE in 2000 for services to financial journalism. He was the joint winner of the Wincott Foundation senior prize for excellence in financial journalism in 1989 and

1997, and winner of the RTZ David Watt Memorial Prize (1994), Ludwig Erhard Prize for economic commentary, and Commentariat of the Year at the Comment Awards (2009). He is the author of four books.

Shoshana Zuboff is the author of *In the Age of the Smart Machine: The Future of Work and Power* and *The Age of Surveillance Capitalism: The Fight for a Human Future at the New Frontier of Power*, a book that integrates her lifelong interests: the digital revolution, the evolution of capitalism, and their shared implications for humanity in the twenty-first century. She is the Charles Edward Wilson Professor emerita at Harvard Business School.

Acknowledgements

As I suggested in my introduction, this book is the fruit of my longstanding partnership with the Burda and DLD teams and wouldn't have come into existence without the help of Paul-Bernhard Kallen, Steffi Czerny, Alexandra Schiel, and Heiko Schlott. Also thanks to Annette Jung for designing the splendid cover. And really special thanks to Burda's Sophie Ahrens – Munich's most patient herder of cats – who, in her quietly authoritative way, has shepherded this project through from podcast beginning to literary end.

On my team, many, many thanks to Nick Humphrey for his outstanding editorial help in putting together this collection at record speed. Thanks to Jason Sanderson for his development of the podcast show, to Jason Alvarez at Literary Hub Radio for keeping it going, and to John Murillo for all his invaluable technological assistance. Thanks also to my literary agent and friend Toby Mundy who managed the trickiest legal issues with his characteristic good humor.

ACKNOWLEDGEMENTS

Thanks to all the folks at Atlantic Books in London, especially CEO Will Atkinson and my long-time editor James Nightingale.

Above all, huge thanks to all my 18 interviewees – the most inspiring tomorrows of today to whom this collection is dedicated.

A note about the editor

Andrew Keen is one of the world's best-known and controversial commentators on the digital revolution. He is the author of four acclaimed and prescient books: *The Cult of the Amateur*, *Digital Vertigo*, *The Internet Is Not the Answer*, and *How to Fix the Future*. He is also a serial tech entrepreneur who has founded many start-ups, including Audiocafe, AfterTV, and the Silicon Valley innovation salon Futurecast.